Leigh Hunt, Reginald Brimely Johnson

Poems

With Prefaces from Some of his Periodicals

Leigh Hunt, Reginald Brimely Johnson

Poems
With Prefaces from Some of his Periodicals

ISBN/EAN: 9783744678032

Printed in Europe, USA, Canada, Australia, Japan

Cover: Foto ©Thomas Meinert / pixelio.de

More available books at **www.hansebooks.com**

The Temple Library

POEMS OF LEIGH HUNT

POEMS

OF

LEIGH HUNT

With prefaces from some of his periodicals

SELECTED AND EDITED

BY

REGINALD BRIMLEY JOHNSON

WITH BIBLIOGRAPHY

AND ETCHINGS BY HERBERT RAILTON

LONDON

J. M. DENT AND CO.

69 GREAT EASTERN STREET

1891

VOL. II.

CONTENTS.

NARRATIVE POEMS.

POLITICAL AND CRITICAL POEMS.

SONNETS.

BLANK VERSE.

ILLUSTRATIONS.

THE STORY OF RIMINI.[1]

Time, the close of the 13th century. Scene, first at Ravenna, afterwards at Rimini.

[Published separately, 1816. In an altered form in "Works," 1832, 1844, 1857, and 1860. "Rimini and other Poems," 1844. "Favourite Poems," 1877. Kent, 1889. "Canterbury Poets," 1889.]

CANTO I.

THE COMING TO FETCH THE BRIDE FROM RAVENNA.

THE sun is up, and 'tis a morn of May
Round old Ravenna's clear-shewn towers and bay,
A morn, the loveliest which the year has seen,
Last of the spring, yet fresh with all its green ;
For a warm eve, and gentle rains at night,
Have left a sparkling welcome for the light,

---

[1] Reprinted from the rare first edition.—ED.

And there's a crystal clearness all about;
The leaves are sharp, the distant hills look out ;
A balmy briskness comes upon the breeze ;
The smoke goes dancing from the cottage trees ;
. And when you listen you may hear a coil
Of bubbling springs about the grassy soil ;
And all the scene in short—sky, and earth, and
    sea—
Breathes like a bright-eyed face, that laughs out
    openly.

'Tis nature, full of spirits, waked and springing :—
The birds to the delicious time are singing,
Darting with freaks and snatches up and down,
Where the light woods go seaward from the town ;
While happy faces, striking through the green
Of leafy roads, at every turn are seen ;
And the far ships, lifting their sails of white
Like joyful hands, come up with scattery light ;
Come gleaming up—true to the wished-for day,
And chase the whistling brine, and swirl into the
    bay.

And well may all who can, come crowding
    there,
If peace returning, and processions rare,
And, to crown all, a marriage in May weather,
Have aught to bring enjoying hearts together ;
For, on this sparkling day, Ravenna's pride,
The daughter of their prince, becomes a bride ;
A bride to crown the comfort of the land ;
And he, whose victories have obtained her hand,
Has taken with the dawn, so flies report,
His promised journey to the expecting court,

With hasting pomp, and squires of high degree,
The bold Giovanni, Lord of Rimini.

Already in the streets the stir grows loud
Of expectation and a bustling crowd.
With feet and voice the gathering hum contends,
The deep talk heaves, the ready laugh ascends ;
Callings, and clapping doors, and curs unite,
And shouts from mere exuberance of delight,
And armed bands, making important way,
Gallant and grave, the lords of holiday,
And nodding neighbours, greeting as they run,
And pilgrims, chanting in the morning sun.
With heaved-out tapestry the windows glow,
By lovely faces brought, that come and go ;
Till, the work smoothed, and all the street attired,
They take their seats, with upward gaze admired ;
Some looking down, some forwards or aside,
As suits the conscious charm in which they pride ;
Some turning a trim waist, or o'er the flow
Of crimson cloths hanging a hand of snow ;
But all with smiles prepared and garlands green,
And all in fluttering talk, impatient for the scene.

And hark ! the approaching trumpets, with a
          start
On the smooth wind, come dancing to the heart.
A moment's hush succeeds ; and from the walls,
Firm and at once, a silver answer calls.
Then heave the crowd ; and all, who best can
          strive
In shuffling struggle, tow'rd the palace drive,
Where balconied and broad, of marble fair,
On pillars it o'erlooks the public square :

For there Duke Guido is to hold his state,
With his fair daughter, seated o'er the gate :—
But the full place rejects the invading tide;
And, after a rude heave from side to side,
With angry faces turned and feet regained,
The peaceful press with order is maintained,
Leaving the doorways only for the crowd,
The space within for the procession proud.

For in this manner is the square set out :—
The sides, path-deep, are crowded round about,
And fac'd with guards, who keep the road entire ;
And opposite to these, a brilliant quire
Of knights and ladies hold the central spot,
Seated in groups upon a grassy plot ;
The seats with boughs are shaded from above
Of early trees transplanted from a grove,
And in the midst, fresh whistling through the
        scene,
A lightsome fountain starts from out the green,
Clear and compact, till, at its height o'errun,
It shakes its loosening silver in the sun.

There, talking with the ladies, you may see,
Standing about, or seated frank and free,
Some of the finest warriors of the court,—
Baptist, and Hugo of the princely port,
And Azo, and Obizo, and the grace
Of frank Esmerield, with his open face,
And Felix the Fine Arm, and him who well
Repays his lavish honours, Lionel ;
Besides a host of spirits, nursed in glory,
Fit for sweet woman's love and for the poet's story.

There, too, in thickest of the bright-eyed
    throng,
Stands the young father of Italian song—
Guy Cavalcanti, of a knightly race ;
The poet looks out in his earnest face :
He with the pheasant's plume—there—bending
    now :
Something he speaks around him with a bow,
And all the listening looks, with nods and flushes,
Break round him into smiles and sparkling
    blushes.

Another start of trumpets, with reply ;
And o'er the gate a sudden canopy
Raises on ivory shafts a crimson shade,
And Guido issues with the princely maid,
And sits ;—the courtiers fall on either side ;
But every look is fixed upon the bride,
Who pensive comes at first, and hardly hears
The enormous shout that springs as she appears ;
Till, as she views the countless gaze below,
And faces that with grateful homage glow,
A home to leave and husband yet to see
Fade in the warmth of that great charity ;
And hard it is, she thinks, to have no will ;
But not to bless these thousands, harder still.
With that, a keen and quivering glance of tears
Scarce moves her patient mouth, and disappears ;
A smile is underneath, and breaks away,
And round she looks and breathes, as best befits
    the day.

What need I tell of lovely lips, and eyes,
A clipsome waist, and bosom's balmy rise ?

The dress of bridal white, and the dark curls
Bedding an airy coronet of pearls?
There's not in all that crowd one gallant being,
Whom if his heart were whole, and rank agreeing,
It would not fire to twice of what he is,
To clasp her to his heart, and call her his.

　While thus with tiptoe looks the people gaze,
Another shout the neighb'ring quarters raise :
The train are in the town, and gathering near
With noise of cavalry and trumpets clear,
A princely music unbedinned with drums ;
The mighty brass seems opening as it comes ;
And now it fills, and now it shakes the air,
And now it bursts into the sounding square ;
At which the crowd with such a shout rejoice,
Each thinks he's deafened with his neighbour's
　　　voice.
Then, with a long-drawn breath, the clangours die,
The palace trumpets give a last reply,
And clattering hoofs succeed, with stately stir
Of snortings proud and clinking furniture :
It seems as if the harnessed war were near ;
But in their garb of peace the train appear,
Their swords alone reserved, but idly hung,
And the chains freed by which their shields were
　　　slung.

　First come the trumpeters, clad all in white,
Except the breast, which wears a scutcheon
　　　bright.
By four and four they ride, on horses gray ;
And as they sit along their easy way,

Stately, and heaving to the sway below,
Each plants his trumpet on his saddle-bow.

The heralds next appear, in vests attired,
Of stiffening gold with radiant colours fired ;
And then the pursuivants, who wait on these,
All dressed in painted richness to the knees :
Each rides a dappled horse, and bears a shield,
Charged with three heads upon a golden field.

Twelve ranks of squires come after, twelve in
        one,
With forked pennons lifted in the sun,
Which tell, as they look backward in the wind,
The bearings of the knights that ride behind.
Their steeds are ruddy bay ; and every squire
His master's colour shows in his attire.

These past, and at a lordly distance come
The knights themselves, and fill the quickening
        hum,
The flower of Rimini.   Apart they ride,
Six in a row, and with a various pride ;
But all as fresh as fancy could desire,
All shapes of gallantry on steeds of fire.

Differing in colour is the knights' array,
The horses, black and chestnut, roan and bay ;—
The horsemen, crimson vested, purple, and white,—
All but the scarlet cloak for every knight ;
Which thrown apart, and hanging loose behind,
Rests on his steed, and ruffles in the wind.
Their caps of velvet have a lightsome fit,
Each with a dancing feather sweeping it,
Tumbling its white against their short dark hair ;

But what is of the most accomplished air,
All wear memorials of their lady's love,
A ribbon, or a scarf, or silken glove,
Some tied about their arm, some at the breast,
Some, with a drag, dangling from the cap's crest.

A suitable attire the horses shew ;
Their golden bits keep wrangling as they go ;
The bridles glance about with gold and gems ;
And the rich housing-cloths, above the hems
Which comb along the ground with golden pegs,
Are half of net, to show the hinder legs.
Some of the cloths themselves are golden thread
With silk enwoven, azure, green, or red ;
Some spotted on a ground of different hue,
As burning stars upon a cloth of blue,—
Or purple smearings with a velvet light
Rich from the glary yellow thickening bright,—
Or a spring green, powdered with April posies,—
Or flush vermilion, set with silver roses :
But all are wide and large, and with the wind,
When it comes fresh, go sweeping out behind.

With various earnestness the crowd admire
Horseman and horse, the motion and the attire.
Some watch, as they go by, the riders' faces
Looking composure, and their knightly graces,
The life, the carelessness, the sudden heed,   .
The body curving to the rearing steed,
The patting hand—that best persuades the check,
And makes the quarrel up with a proud neck.
The thigh broad pressed, the spanning palm
          upon it,
And the jerked feather swaling in the bonnet.

Others the horses and their pride explore,
Their jauntiness behind and strength before ;
The flowing back, firm chest, and fetlocks clean,
The branching veins ridging the glossy lean,
The mane hung sleekly, the projecting eye
That to the stander near looks awfully,
The finished head, in its compactness free,
Small, and o'erarching to the lifted knee,
The start and snatch, as if they felt the comb,
With mouths that fling about the creamy foam.—
The snorting turbulence, the nod, the champing,
The shift, the tossing, and the fiery tramping.

And now the Princess, pale and with fixed eye,
Perceives the last of those precursors nigh,
Each rank uncovering as they pass in state,
Both to the courtly fountain and the gate ;
And then a second interval succeeds
Of stately length, and then a troop of steeds
Milk-white and unattired, Arabian bred,
Each by a blooming boy lightsomely led :
In every limb is seen their faultless race,
A fire well-temper'd, and a free left grace :
Slender their spotless shapes, and meet the sight
With freshness, after all those colours bright ;
And as with quoit-like drop their steps they bear,
They lend their streaming tails to the fond air.
These for a princely present are divined,
And show the giver is not far behind.

The talk increases now, and now advance
Space after space, with many a sprightly prance,
The pages of the court, in rows of three ;
Of white and crimson is their livery.

Space after space, and yet the attendants come,
And deeper goes about the impatient hum—
Ah—yes—no ! 'tis not he, but 'tis the squires
Who go before him when his pomp requires.
And now his huntsman shows the lessening train,
Now the squire-carver, and the chamberlain,—
And now his banner comes, and now his shield,
Borne by the squire that waits him to the field ;
And then an interval,—a lordly space ;—
A pin-drop silence strikes o'er all the place.
The princess, from a distance, scarcely knows
Which way to look ; her colour comes and goes,
And with an impulse and affection free,
She lays her hand upon her father's knee,
Who looks upon her with a laboured smile,
Gathering it up into his own the while,
When some one's voice, as if it knew not how
To check itself, exclaims, " The prince ! now,
    now ! "
And on a milk-white courser, like the air,
A glorious figure springs into the square :
Up, with a burst of thunder, goes the shout,
And rolls the trembling walls and peopled roofs
    about.

  Never was nobler finish of fine sight,
'Twas like the coming of a shape of light ;
And every lovely gazer, with a start,
Felt the quick pleasure smite across her heart :—
The princess, who at first could scarcely see,
Though looking still that way from dignity,
Gathers new courage as the praise goes round,
And bends her eyes to learn what they have found.

And see—his horse obeys the check unseen,
And, with an air 'twixt ardent and serene,
Letting a fall of curls about his brow,
He takes his cap off with a gallant bow.
Then for another, and a deafening shout,
And scarfs are waved, and flowers come fluttering
    out ;
And, shaken by the noise, the reeling air   ⎫[1]
Sweeps with a giddy whirl among the fair,   ⎬
And whisks their garments and their shining ⎪
    hair.   ⎭

With busy interchange of wonder glows
The crowd, and loves his brilliance as he goes,—
The golden-fretted cap, the downward feather,—
The crimson vest fitting with pearls together,—
The rest in snowy white from the mid thigh :
These catch the extrinsic and the common eye :
But on his shape the gentler sight attends,
Moves as he passes,—as he bends him, bends,—
Watches his air, his gesture, and his face,
And thinks it never saw such manly grace ;
So fine are his bare throat, and curls of black,—
So lightsomely dropt in, his lordly back,—
His thigh so fitted for the tilt or dance,
So heaped with strength, and turned with elegance ;
But, above all, so meaning is his look,
Full, and as readable as open book ;
And so much easy dignity there lies

---

1 " I confess I like the very bracket that marks out the triplet to the reader's eye, and prepares him for the music of it. It has a look like the bridge of a lute."—Preface to " Works," 1832.

In the frank lifting of his cordial eyes.

His haughty steed, who seems by turns to be
Vexed and made proud by that cool mastery,
Shakes at his bit, and rolls his eyes with care,
Reaching with stately step at the fine air;
And now and then, sideling his restless pace,
Drops with his hinder legs, and shifts his place,
And feels through all his frame a fiery thrill ;
The princely rider on his back sits still,
And looks where'er he likes, and sways him at
    his will.

Surprise, relief, a joy scarce understood,
Something perhaps of very gratitude,
And fifty feelings undefin'd and new,
Dance through the bride, and flush her faded hue.
"Could I but once," she thinks, "securely place
A trust for the contents on such a case,
And know the spirit that should fill that dwelling,
This chance of mine would hardly be compelling."
Just then, the stranger, coming slowly round
By the clear fountain and the brilliant ground,
And bending, as he goes, with frequent thanks,
Beckons a follower to him from the ranks,
And loosening, as he speaks, from its light hold,
A dropping jewel with its chain of gold,
Sends it, in token he had loved him long,
To the young master of Italian song.
The youth smiles up, and with a lowly grace
Bending his lifted eyes and blushing face,
Looks after his new friend, who scarcely gone
In the wide turning, nods and passes on.

This is sufficient for the destined bride :
She took an interest first, but now a pride ;
And as the prince comes riding to the place,
Baring his head, and raising his fine face,
She meets his full obeisance with an eye
Of self-permission and sweet gravity ;
He looks with touched respect, and gazes and
     goes by.

CANTO II.

THE BRIDE'S JOURNEY TO RIMINI.

We'll pass the followers, and their closing state ;
The court was entered by an hinder gate ;
The duke and princess had retired before,
Joined by the knights and ladies at the door ;
But something seemed amiss, and there ensued
Deep talk among the spreading multitude,
Who got in clumps, or paced the measured street,
Filling with earnest hum the noontide heat.
Nor ceased the wonder, as the day increased,
And brought no symptoms of a bridal feast,
No mass, no tilt, no largess for the crowd,
Nothing to answer that procession proud,
But a blank look, as if no court had been—
Silence without, and secrecy within ;
And nothing heard by listening at the walls,
But now and then a bustling through the halls,
Or the dim organ roused at gathering intervals.

    The truth was this :—The bridegroom had not
     come,

But sent his brother, proxy in his room.
A lofty spirit the former was, and proud,
Little gallant, and had a sort of cloud
Hanging forever on his cold address,
Which he mistook for proper manliness :—
But more of this hereafter.   Guido knew
The prince's character ; and he knew, too,
That sweet as was his daughter, and prepared
To do her duty where appeal was barred,
She had stout notions on the marrying score,
And where the match unequal prospect bore,
Might pause with firmness, and refuse to strike
A chord her own sweet music so unlike.
The old man therefore, kind enough at heart,
Yet fond from habit of intrigue and art,
And little formed for sentiments like these
Which seemed to him mere maiden niceties,
Had thought at once to gratify the pride
Of his stern neighbour, and secure the bride,
By telling him, that if, as he had heard,
Busy he was just then, 'twas but a word,
And he might send and wed her by another—
Of course, no less a person than his brother.
The bride meantime was told, and not unmoved,
To look for one no sooner seen than loved ;
And when Giovanni, struck with what he
     thought
Mere proof how his triumphant hand was sought,
Despatched the wished-for prince, who was a
     creature
Formed in the very poetry of nature,
The effect was perfect, and the future wife
Caught in the elaborate snare, perhaps for life.

One shock there was, however, to sustain,
Which nigh restored her to herself again.
She saw, when all were housed, in Guido's face
A look of leisurely surprise take place ;
A little whispering followed for awhile,
And then 'twas told her with an easy smile,
That Prince Giovanni, to his great chagrin,
Had been delayed by something unforeseen,
But rather than delay his day of bliss,
(If his fair ruler took it not amiss,)
Had sent his brother Paulo in his stead ;
"Who," said old Guido, with a nodding head,
"May well be said to represent his brother,
For when you see the one, you know the other."

By this time Paulo joined them where they stood,
And, seeing her in some uneasy mood,
Changed the mere cold respects his brother sent
To such a strain of cordial compliment,
And paid them with an air so frank and bright,
As to a friend appreciated at sight,
That air, in short, which sets you at your ease
Without implying your perplexities,
That what with the surprise in every way,
The hurry of the time, the appointed day,
The very shame which now appeared increased
Of begging leave to have her hand released,
And above all, those tones, and smiles, and looks,
Which seemed to realize the dreams of books,
And helped her genial fancy to conclude
That fruit of such a stock must all be good,
She knew not how to object in her confusion ;
Quick were the marriage rites ; and, in conclusion,

The proxy, turning 'mid the general hush,
Kissed her meek lips, betwixt a rosy blush.

At last about the vesper hour, a score
Of trumpets issued from the palace door,
The banners of their brass with favours tied,
And with a blast proclaimed the wedded bride,
But not a word the sullen silence broke,
Till something of a gift the herald spoke,
And with a bag of money issuing out,
Scattered the ready harvest round about ;
Then burst the mob into a jovial cry,
And " largess! largess!" claps against the sky, }
And bold Giovanni's name, the lord of Rimini. }

The rest however still were looking on,
Careless and mute, and scarce the noise was gone,
When riding from the gate with banners reared,
Again the morning visitors appeared.
The prince was in his place ; and in a car,
Before him, glistening like a farewell star,
Sate the dear lady with her brimming eyes,
And off they set, through doubtful looks and cries;
For some too shrewdly guessed, and some were
        vexed
At the dull day, and some the whole perplexed,
And all great pity thought it to divide
Two that seemed made for bridegroom and for
        bride.
Ev'n she, whose heart this strange, abrupt event
Had seared as 'twere with burning wonderment,
Could scarce at times a passionate cry forbear
At leaving her own home and native air ;

Till passing now the limits of the town,
And on the last few gazers looking down,
She saw by the road-side an aged throng,
Who wanting power to bustle with the strong,
Had learnt their gracious mistress was to go,
And gathered there, an unconcerted show.
Bending they stood, with their old foreheads bare,
And the winds fingered with their reverend hair.
Farewell, farewell, my friends ! she would have
    cried,
But in her throat the leaping accents died,
And, waving with her hand a vain adieu,
She dropt her veil, and backwarder withdrew,
And let the kindly tears their own good course
    pursue.

It was a lovely evening, fit to close
A lovely day, and brilliant in repose;
Warm, but not dim, a glow was in the air ;
The softened breeze came smoothing here and there ;
And every tree, in passing, one by one,
Gleamed out with twinkles of the golden sun :
For leafy was the road, with tall array,
On either side, of mulberry and bay,
And distant snatches of blue hills between;
And there the alder was with its bright green,
And the broad chestnut, and the poplar's shoot,
That like a feather waves from head to foot,
With, ever and anon, majestic pines ;
And still from tree to tree the early vines
Hung garlanding the way in amber lines.

Nor long the princess kept her from the view
Of that dear scenery with its parting hue ;

II.   C

For sitting now, calm from the gush of tears,
With dreaming eye fixed down, and half-shut ears,
Hearing, yet hearing not, the fervent sound
Of hoofs thick reckoning and the wheel's moist
    round,
A call of " slower ! " from the farther part
Of the checked riders, woke her with a start,
And looking up again, half sigh, half stare,
She lifts her veil, and feels the freshening air.

'Tis down a hill they go, gentle indeed,
And such, as with a bold and pranksome speed
Another time they would have scorned to ⎞
    measure;   ⎟
But now they take with them a lovely treasure, ⎬
And feel they should consult her gentle pleasure. ⎠

And now with thicker shades the pines appear ;—
The noise of hoofs grows duller to her ear ;
And quitting suddenly their gravelly toil,
The wheels go spinning o'er a sandy soil.
Here first the silence of the country seems
To come about her with its listening dreams,
And full of anxious thoughts, half-freed from pain,
In downward musing she relapsed again ;
Leaving the others, who had passed that way
In careless spirits of the early day,
To look about, and mark the reverend scene,
For awful tales renowned and everlasting green.

A heavy spot the forest looks at first,
To one grim shade condemned, and sandy thirst,
Or only chequered, here and there, with bushes,
Dusty and sharp, or plashy pools with rushes,

About whose sides the swarming insects fry,
Opening with noisome din, as they go by ;
But, entering more and more, they quit the sand
At once, and strike upon a grassy land,
From which the trees, as from a carpet, rise
In knolls and clumps, with rich varieties.
A moment's trouble find the knights to rein
Their horses in, which, feeling turf again,
Thrill, and curvet, and long to be at large
To scour the space, and give the winds a charge,
Or pulling tight the bridles as they pass,
Dip their warm mouths into the freshening grass :
But soon in easy rank, from glade to glade,
Proceed they, coasting underneath the shade ;
Some baring to the cool their placid brows,
Some looking upward through the glimmering
        boughs,
Or peering grave through inward-opening places,
And half prepared for glimpse of shadowy faces.
Various the trees and passing foliage here,—
Wild pear, and oak, and dusky juniper,
With briony between in trails of white,
And ivy, and the suckle's streaky light,
And, moss, warm gleaming with a sudden mark,
Like flings of sunshine left upon the bark ;
And still the pine, long-haired and dark, and tall,
In lordly right, predominant o'er all.

    Much they admire that old religious tree
With shaft above the rest up-shooting free,
And shaking, when its dark locks feel the wind,
Its wealthy fruit with rough Mosaic rind.
At noisy intervals, the living cloud

Of cawing rooks breaks o'er them, gathering loud
Like a wild people at a stranger's coming;
Then hushing paths succeed, with insects humming,
Or ring-dove that repeats his pensive plea,
Or startled gull up-screaming tow'rds the sea.
But scarce their eyes encounter living thing
Save, now and then, a goat loose wandering,
Or a few cattle looking up aslant
With sleepy eyes, and meek mouths ruminant,
Or once, a plodding woodman, old and bent,
Passing, with half-indifferent wonderment,
Yet turning at the last to look once more;
Then feels his trembling staff, and onward as
    before.

So ride they pleased;—till now the couching
    sun
Levels his final look through shadows dun;
And the clear moon, with meek o'er-lifted face,
Seems come to look into the silvering place.
Then woke the bride indeed, for then was heard,
Sole voice, the poet's and the lover's bird,
Preluding first, as if the sounds were cast
For the dear leaves about her, till at last
With shot-out raptures, in a perfect shower,
She vents her heart on the delicious hour.
Lightly the horsemen go, as if they'd ride
A velvet path, and hear no voice beside :
A placid hope assures the breath-suspended
    bride.

So ride they in delight through beam and shade;—
Till many a rill now passed, and many a glade,

They quit the piny labyrinths, and soon
Emerge into the full and sheeted moon :
Chilling it seems ; and pushing steed on steed,
They start them freshly with a homeward speed.
Then well-known fields they pass, and straggling
cots,
Boy-storied trees, and passion-plighted spots,
And turning last a sudden corner, see
The square-lit towers of slumbering Rimini.
The marble bridge comes heaving forth below
With a long gleam ; and nearer as they go,
They see the still Marecchia, cold and bright,
Sleeping along with face against the light.
A hollow trample now,—a fall of chains,—
The bride has entered,—not a voice remains ;—
Night, and a maiden silence, wrap the plains.

CANTO III.

THE FATAL PASSION.

Now why must I disturb a dream of bliss,
Or bring cold sorrow 'twixt the wedded kiss ?
Sad is the strain, with which I cheer my long
And caged hours, and try my native tongue ; [1]
Now too, while rains autumnal, as I sing,
Wash the dull bars, chilling my sicklied wing,
And all the climate presses on my sense ;
But thoughts it furnishes of things far hence,
And leafy dreams affords me, and a feeling

[1] The preceding canto, and a small part of the present,
were written in prison.

Which I should else disdain, tear-dipped and
    healing ;
And shews me,—more than what it first de-
    signed,—
How little upon earth our home we find,
Or close the intended course of erring human
    kind.

Enough of this. Yet how shall I disclose
The weeping days that with the morning rose,
How bring the bitter disappointment in,—
The holy cheat, the virtue-binding sin,—
The shock, that told this lovely, trusting heart,
That she had given, beyond all power to part,
Her hope, belief, love, passion, to one brother,
Possession (oh, the misery !) to another !

Some likeness was there 'twixt the two,—an air
At times, a cheek, a colour of the hair,
A tone, when speaking of indifferent things ;
Nor, by the scale of common measurings,
Would you say more perhaps, than that the one
Was more robust, the other finelier spun ;
That of the two, Giovanni was the graver,
Paulo the livelier, and the more in favour.

Some tastes there were indeed, that would prefer
Giovanni's countenance as the martialler ;
And 'twas a soldier's truly, if an eye
Ardent and cool at once, drawn-back and high,
An eagle's nose, and a determined lip,
Were the best marks of manly soldiership.
Paulo's was fashioned in a different mould,
And finer still, I think ; for though 'twas bold,

When boldness was required, and could put on
A glowing frown, as if an angel shone,
Yet there was nothing in it one might call
A stamp exclusive, or professional :
No courtier's face, and yet its smile was ready,—
No scholar's, yet its look was deep and steady,—
No soldier's, for its power was all of mind,
Too true for violence, and too refined.
A graceful nose was his, lightsomely brought
Down from a forehead of clear-spirited thought ;
Wisdom looked sweet and inward from his eye ;
And round his mouth was sensibility :—
It was a face, in short, seemed made to shew
How far the genuine flesh and blood could go ;—
A morning glass of unaffected nature,—
Something that baffled every pompous feature,—
The visage of a glorious human creature.

If any points there were, at which they came
Nearer together, 'twas in knightly fame,
And all accomplishments that art may know,—
Hunting, and princely hawking, and the bow,
The rush together in the bright-eyed list,
Fore-thoughted chess, the riddle rarely missed,
And the decision of still knottier points,
With knife in hand, of boar and peacock joints,—
Things that might shake the fame that Tristram got,
And bring a doubt on perfect Launcelot,
But leave we knighthood to the former part ;
The tale I tell is of the human heart.

The worst of Prince Giovanni, as his bride
Too quickly found, was an ill-tempered pride.

Bold, handsome, able if he chose to please,
Punctual and right in common offices,
He lost the sight of conduct's only worth,
The scattering smiles on this uneasy earth,
And on the strength of virtues of small weight,
Claimed tow'rds himself the exercise of great.
He kept no reckoning with his sweets and sours ;—
He'd hold a sullen countenance for hours,
And then, if pleased to cheer himself a space,
Look for the immediate rapture in your face,
And wonder that a cloud could still be there,
How small soever, when his own was fair.
Yet such is conscience,—so design'd to keep
Stern, central watch, though all things else go
    sleep,
And so much knowledge of one's self there lies
Cored, after all, in our complacencies,
That no suspicion would have touched him
    more
Than that of wanting on the generous score :
He would have whelmed you with a weight of
    scorn,
Been proud at eve, inflexible at morn,
In short, ill-tempered for a week to come,
And all to strike that desperate error dumb.
Taste had he, in a word, for high-turned merit,
But not the patience or the genial spirit ;
And so he made, 'twixt virtue and defect,
A sort of fierce demand on your respect,
Which, if assisted by his high degree,
It gave him in some eyes a dignity,
And struck a meaner deference in the many,
Left him, at last, unloveable with any.

From this complexion in the reigning brother,
His younger birth perhaps had saved the other.
Born to a homage less gratuitous,
He learned to win a nobler for his house ;
And both from habit and a genial heart,
Without much trouble of the reasoning art,
Found this the wisdom and the sovereign good,—
To be, and make, as happy as he could.
Not that he saw, or thought he saw, beyond
His general age, and could not be as fond
Of wars and creeds as any of his race,
But most he loved a happy human face ;
And wheresoe'er his fine, frank eyes were thrown,
He struck the looks he wished for with his own.
His danger was, lest; feeling as he did,
Too lightly he might leap o'er means forbid,
And in some tempting hour lose sight of crime
O'er some sweet face too happy for the time ;
But fears like these he never entertained,
And had they crossed him, would have been dis-
        dained.
Warm was his youth, 'tis true,—nor had been
        free
From lighter loves,—but virtue reverenced he,
And had been kept from men of pleasure's cares
By dint of feelings still more warm than theirs.
So what but service leaped where'er he went !
Was there a tilt-day or a tournament,—
For welcome grace there rode not such an-
        other,
Nor yet for strength, except his lordly brother.
Was there a court-day, or a sparkling feast,
Or better still,—in my ideas, at least,—

A summer party to the greenwood shade,
With lutes prepared, and cloth on herbage laid,
And ladies' laughter coming through the air,—
He was the readiest and the blithest there ;
And made the time so exquisitely pass
With stories told with elbow on the grass,
Or touched the music in his turn so finely,
That all he did, they thought, was done divinely.

The lovely stranger could not fail to see
Too soon this difference, more especially
As her consent, too lightly now, she thought,
With hopes far different had been strangely
      bought ;
And many a time the pain of that neglect
Would strike in blushes o'er her self-respect ;
But since the ill was cureless, she applied
With busy virtue to resume her pride,
And hoped to value her submissive heart
On playing well a patriot daughter's part,
Trying her new-found duties to prefer
To what a father might have owed to her.
The very day too, when her first surprise
Was full, kind tears had come into her eyes
On finding, by his care, her private room
Furnished, like magic, from her own at home ;
The very books and all transported there,
The leafy tapestry, and the crimson chair,
The lute, the glass that told the shedding hours,
The little urn of silver for the flowers,
The frame for broidering, with a piece half done,
And the white falcon, basking in the sun,
Who, when he saw her, sidled on his stand,

And twined his neck against her trembling hand.
But what had touched her nearest, was the
    thought,
That if 'twere destined for her to be brought
To a sweet mother's bed, the joy would be
Giovanni's too, and his her family :—
He seemed already father of her child,
And in the nestling pledge in patient thought she
    smiled.
Yet then a pang would cross her, and the red
In either downward cheek startle and spread,
To think that he, who was to have such part
In joys like these, had never shared her heart ;
But back she chased it with a sigh austere ;
And did she chance, 'at times like these, to hear
Her husband's footstep, she would haste the
    more,
And with a double smile open the door,
And ask him after all his morning's doing,
Had his new soldiers pleased him in reviewing,
Or if the boar was slain, which he had been
    pursuing.

    The prince at this, would bend on her an eye
Cordial enough, and kiss her tenderly ;
Nor, to say truly, was he slow in common
To accept the attentions of this lovely woman ;
But then meantime he took no generous pains,
By mutual pleasing, to secure his gains ;
He entered not, in turn, in her delights,
Her books, her flowers, her taste for rural sights ;
Nay, scarcely her sweet singing minded he,
Unless his pride was roused by company ;

Or when to please him, after martial play,
She strained her lute to some old fiery lay
Of fierce Orlando, or of Ferumbras,
Or Ryan's cloak, or how by the red grass
In battle you might know where Richard was.

Yet all the while, no doubt, however stern
Or cold at heart, he thought he loved in turn,
And that the joy he took in her sweet ways,
The pride he felt when she excited praise,
In short, the enjoyment of his own good pleasure,
Was thanks enough, and passion beyond measure.

She, had she loved him, might have thought so
    too :
For what will love's exalting not go through,
Till long neglect, and utter selfishness,
Shew the fond pride it takes in its distress ?
But ill prepared was she, in her hard lot,
To fancy merit, where she found it not,—
She who had been beguiled,—she, who was made
Within a gentle bosom to be laid,—
To bless and to be blessed,—to be heart-bare
To one who found his bettered likeness there,—
To think for ever with him, like a bride,—
To haunt his eye, like taste personified,—
To double his delight, to share his sorrow,
And like a morning beam, wake to him every
    morrow.

Paulo, meantime, who ever since the day
He saw her sweet looks bending o'er his way,
Had stored them up, unconsciously, as graces
By which to judge all other forms and faces,

Had learnt, I know not how, the secret snare,
That gave her up, that evening, to his care.
Some babbler, may-be, of old Guido's court,
Or foolish friend had told him, half in sport;
But to his heart the fatal flattery went;
And grave he grew, and inwardly intent,
And ran back, in his mind, with sudden spring,
Look, gesture, smile, speech, silence, everything,
Even what before had seemed indifference,
And read them over in another sense.
Then would he blush with sudden self-disdain,
To think how fanciful he was, and vain ;
And with half angry, half regretful sigh,
Tossing his chin, and feigning a free eye,
Breathe off, as 'twere, the idle tale, and look
About him for his falcon or his book ;
Scorning that ever he should entertain
One thought that in the end might give his brother
    pain.

    This start, however, came so often round,—
So often fell he in deep thought, and found
Occasion to renew his carelessness,
Yet every time the power grown less and less,
That by degrees, half wearied, half inclined,
To the sweet struggling image he resigned ;
And merely, as he thought, to make the best
Of what by force would come about his breast,
Began to bend down his admiring eyes
On all her touching looks and qualities,
Turning their shapely sweetness every way,
Till 'twas his food and habit day by day,
And she became companion of his thought ;—

Silence her gentleness before him brought,
Society her sense, reading her books,
Music her voice, every sweet thing her looks,
Which sometimes seemed, when he sat fixed awhile,
To steal beneath his eyes with upward smile:
And did he stroll into some lonely place,
Under the trees, upon the thick soft grass,
How charming, would he think, to see her here!
How heightened then, and perfect would appear
The two divinest things this world has got,
A lovely woman in a rural spot!

Thus daily went he on, gathering sweet pain
About his fancy, till it thrilled again;
And if his brother's image, less and less,
Startled him up from his new idleness,
'Twas not—he fancied—that he reasoned worse,
Or felt less scorn of wrong, but the reverse.
That we should think of injuring another,
Or trenching on his peace,—this too a brother,—
And all from selfishness and pure weak will,
To him seemed marvellous and impossible.
'Tis true, thought he, one being more there was,
Who might meantime have weary hours to pass,—
One weaker too to bear them,—and for whom?—
No matter;—he could not reverse her doom;
And so he sighed and smiled, as if one thought
Of paltering could suppose that *he* was to be caught.

Yet if she loved him, common gratitude,
If not, a sense of what was fair and good,
Besides his new relationship and right,
Would make him wish to please her all he might;

And as to thinking,—where could be the harm,
If to his heart he kept its secret charm?
He wished not to himself another's blessing,
But then he might console for not possessing;
And glorious things there were, which but to see
And not admire, was mere stupidity:
He might as well object to his own eyes
For loving to behold the fields and skies,
His neighbour's grove, or story-painted hall;
'Twas but the taste for what was natural;
Only his fav'rite thought was loveliest of them all.
Concluding thus, and happier that he knew
His ground so well, near and more near he drew;
And sanctioned by his brother's manner, spent
Hours by her side as happy as well-meant.
He read with her, he rode, he went a hawking,
He spent still evenings in delightful talking,
While she sat busy at her broidery frame;
Or touched the lute with her, and when they came
To some fine part, prepared her for the pleasure,
And then with double smile stole on the measure.

Then at the tournament,—who there but she
Made him more gallant still than formerly,
Couch o'er his tightened lance with double force,
Pass like the wind, sweeping down man and horse,
And franklier then than ever, 'midst the shout
And dancing trumpets ride, uncovered, round
    about?
His brother only, more than hitherto,
He would avoid, or sooner let subdue,
Partly from something strange unfelt before,
Partly because Giovanni sometimes wore

A knot his bride had worked him, green and gold ;—
For in all things with nature did she hold ;
And while 'twas being worked, her fancy was
Of sunbeams mingling with a tuft of grass.

Francesca from herself but ill could hide
What pleasure now was added to her side,—
How placidly, yet fast, the days succeeded
With one who thought and felt so much as she
     did,—
And how the chair he sat in, and the room,
Began to look, when he had failed to come.
But as she better knew the cause than he,
She seemed to have the more necessity
For struggling hard, and rousing all her pride ;
And so she did at first ; she even tried
To feel a sort of anger at his care ;
But these extremes brought but a kind despair ;
And then she only spoke more sweetly to him,
And found her failing eyes give looks that melted
     through him.

Giovanni too, who felt relieved indeed
To see another to his place succeed,
Or rather filling up some trifling hours
Better spent elsewhere, and beneath his powers,
Left the new tie to strengthen day by day,
Talked less and less, and longer kept away,
Secure in his self love, and sense of right,
That he was welcome most, come when he might.
And doubtless they, in their still finer sense,
With added care repaid this confidence,
Turning their thoughts from his abuse of it,
To what on their own parts was graceful and was fit.

Ah now, ye gentle pair,—now think awhile,
Now, while ye still can think, and still can smile ;
Now, while your generous hearts have not been
    grieved
Perhaps with something not to be retrieved,
And ye have still, within, the power of gladness,
From self-resentment free, and retrospective mad-
    ness !

So did they think ;—but partly from delay,
Partly from fancied ignorance of the way,
And most from feeling the bare contemplation
Give them fresh need of mutual consolation,
They scarcely tried to see each other less,
And did but meet with deeper tenderness,
Living, from day to day, as they were used,
Only with graver thoughts, and smiles reduced,
And sighs more frequent, which, when one would
    heave,
The other longed to start up and receive.
For whether some suspicions now had crossed
Giovanni's mind, or whether he had lost
More of his temper lately, he would treat
His wife with petty scorns, and starts of heat,
And to his own omissions proudly blind,
O'erlook the pains she took to make him kind,
And yet be angry, if he thought them less ;
He found reproaches in her meek distress,
Forcing her silent tears, and then resenting,
Then almost angrier grown from half repenting,
And hinting at the last, that some there were
Better perhaps than he, and tastefuller,
And these, for what he knew,—he little cared,—

II.   D

Might please her, and be pleased, though he
    despaired.
Then would he quit the room, and half disdain
Himself for being in so harsh a strain,
And venting thus his temper on a woman ;
Yet not the more for that changed he in common,
Or took more pains to please her, and be near :—
What ! should he truckle to a woman's tear ?

At times like these the princess tried to shun
The face of Paulo as too kind a one ;
And shutting up her tears with resolute sigh,
Would walk into the air, and see the sky,
And feel about her all the garden green,
And hear the birds that shot the covert boughs
    between.

A noble range it was, of many a rood,
Walled round with trees, and ending in a wood :
Indeed the whole was leafy ; and it had
A winding stream about [it], clear and glad,
That danced from shade to shade, and on its way
Seemed smiling with delight to feel the day.
There was the pouting rose, both red and white,
The flaring heart's-ease, flushed with purple light,
Blush-hiding strawberry, sunny-coloured box,
Hyacinth, handsome with his clustering locks,
The lady lily, looking gently down,
Pure lavender, to lay in bridal gown,
The daisy, lovely on both sides ;—in short,
All the sweet cups to which the bees resort,
With plots of grass, and perfumed walks between
Of citron, honeysuckle, and jessamine,

With orange, whose warm leaves so finely suit,
And look as if they'd shade a golden fruit ;
And 'midst the flow'rs, turfed round beneath a
    shade
Of circling pines, a babbling fountain played,
And 'twixt their shafts you saw the water bright,
Which through the darksome tops glimmered with
    showering light.
So now you walked beside an odorous bed
Of gorgeous hues, white, azure, golden, red ;
And now turned off into a leafy walk
Close and continuous, fit for lovers' talk ;
And now pursued the stream, and as you trod
Onward and onward o'er the velvet sod,
Felt on your face an air, watery and sweet,
And a new sense in your soft-lighting feet.
And then, perhaps, you entered upon shades
Pillowed with dells and uplands 'twixt the glades,
Through which the distant palace now and then
Looked lordly forth with many-windowed ken ;
A land of trees, which reaching round about
In shady blessing stretched their old arms out ;
With spots of sunny opening, and with nooks
To lie and read in, sloping into brooks,
Where at her drink you startled the slim deer,
Retreating lightly with a lovely fear.
And all about, the birds kept leafy house,
And sung and sparkled in and out the boughs ;
And all about, a lovely sky of blue
Clearly was felt, or down the leaves laughed
    through ;
And here and there, in every part, were seats,
Some in the open walks, some in retreats ;

With bowering leaves o'erhead, to which the eye
Look'd up half sweetly and half awfully,—
Places of nestling green, for poets made,
Where, when the sunshine struck a yellow shade,
The slender trunks, to inward peeping sight,
Thronged in dark pillars up the gold green light.

But 'twixt the wood and flowery walks, half-way,
And formed of both, the loveliest portion lay;
A spot, that struck you like enchanted ground :—
It was a shallow dell, set in a mound
Of sloping shrubs that mounted by degrees
The birch and poplar mixed with heavier trees;
From under which, sent through a marble spout,
Betwixt the dark wet green, a rill gushed out,
Whose low sweet talking seemed as if it said
Something eternal to that happy shade:
The ground within was lawn, with plots of flowers
Heaped   towards   the   centre,   and   with   citron
          bowers ;
And in the midst of all, clustered about,
With bay and myrtle, and just gleaming out,
Lurked a pavilion, a delicious sight,—
Small, marble, well-proportioned, mellowy white,
With yellow vine-leaves sprinkled,—but no more,—
And a young orange either side the door.
The door was to the wood, forward and square,
The rest was domed at top and circular ;
And through the dome the only light came in,
Tinged as it entered, with the vine-leaves thin.

It was a beauteous piece of ancient skill,
Spared from the rage of war, and perfect still ;

By most supposed the work of fairy hands,—
Famed for luxurious taste, and choice of lands,
Alcina or Morgana,—who from fights
And errant fame inveigled amorous knights,
And lived with them in a long round of blisses,
Feasts, concerts, baths, and bower-enshaded kisses.
But 'twas a temple, as its sculpture told,
Built to the Nymphs that haunted there of old ;
For o'er the door was carved a sacrifice
By girls and shepherds brought, with reverent eyes,
Of sylvan drinks and foods, simple and sweet,
And goats with struggling horns and planted feet :
And, on a line with this, ran round about,
A like relief, touched exquisitely out,
That showed, in various scenes, the nymphs them-
　　selves ;
Some by the water-side, on bowery shelves
Leaning at will,—some in the water sporting,
With sides half swelling forth, and looks of
　　courting;—
Some in a flowery dell, hearing a swain
Play on his pipe, till the hills ring again,—
Some tying up their long moist hair, some sleeping
Under the trees, with fauns and satyrs peeping,—
Or, sidelong-eyed, pretending not to see
The latter in the brakes come creepingly,
While their forgotten urns, lying about
In the green herbage, let the water out.
Never, be sure, before or since was seen
A summer-house so fine in such a nest of green.

　　All the green garden, flower-bed, shade and plot,
Francesca loved, but most of all this spot.

Whenever she walked forth, wherever went
About the grounds, to this at last she bent :
Here she had brought a lute and a few books ;
Here would she lie for hours, with grateful looks
Thanking at heart the sunshine and the leaves,
The summer rain-drops counting from the eaves,
And all that promising, calm smile we see
In nature's face, when we look patiently.
Then would she think of heaven ; and you might
          hear
Sometimes, when everything was hushed and
          clear,
Her gentle voice from out those shades emerging,
Singing the evening anthem to the Virgin.
The gardeners, and the rest, who served the place,
And blest whenever they beheld her face,
Knelt when they heard it, bowing and uncovered,
And felt as if in air some sainted beauty hovered.

    One day,—'twas on a summer afternoon,
When airs and gurgling brooks are best in tune,
And grasshoppers are loud, and day-work done,
And shades have heavy outlines in the sun,—
The princess came to her accustomed bower
To get her, if she could, a soothing hour ;
Trying, as she was used, to leave her cares
Without, and slumberously enjoy the airs,
And the low-talking leaves, and that cool light ·
The vines let in, and all that hushing sight
Of closing wood seen through the opening door,
And distant plash of waters tumbling o'er,
And smell of citron blooms, and fifty luxuries
          more.

She tried as usual for the trial's sake,
For even that diminished her heart-ache ;
And never yet, how ill soe'er at ease,
Came she for nothing 'midst the flowers and trees.
Yet somehow or another, on that day
She seemed to feel too lightly borne away,—
Too much relieved,—too much inclined to draw
A careless joy from everything she saw,
And looking round her with a new-born eye,
As if some tree of knowledge had been nigh,
To taste of nature primitive and free,
And bask at ease in her heart's liberty.

Painfully clear those rising thoughts appeared,
With something dark at bottom that she feared :
And snatching from the fields her thoughtful look,
She reached o'erhead, and took her down a book,
And fell to reading with as fixed an air,
As though she had been wrapt since morning
        there.

    'Twas "Launcelot of the Lake," a bright ro-
        mance,
That like a trumpet made young pulses dance,
Yet had a softer note that shook still more:—
She had begun it but the day before,
And read with a full heart, half sweet, half sad,
How old King Ban was spoiled of all he had
But one fair castle: how one summer's day
With his fair queen and child he went away
To ask the great King Arthur for assistance ;
How reaching by himself a hill at distance
He turned to give his castle a last look,
And saw its far white face ; and how a smoke

As he was looking, burst in volumes forth,
And good King Ban saw all that he was worth,
And his fair castle.burning to the ground,
So that his wearied pulse felt over-wound,
And he lay down, and said a prayer apart
For those he loved, and broke his poor old heart.
Then read she of the queen with her young child,
How she came up, and nearly had gone wild,
And how in journeying on in her despair,
She reached a lake, and met a lady there,
Who pitied her, and took the baby sweet
Into her arms, when lo, with closing feet
She sprang up all at once, like bird from brake,
And vanished with him underneath the lake.
The mother's feelings we as well may pass :—
The fairy of the place that lady was,
And Launcelot (so the boy was called) became
Her inmate, till in search of knightly fame
He went to Arthur's court, and played his part
So rarely, and displayed so frank a heart,
That what with all-his charms of look and limb,
The Queen Geneura fell in love with him :—
And here, with growing interest in her reading,
The princess, doubly fixed, was now proceeding.

Ready she sat with one hand to turn o'er
The leaf, to which her thoughts ran on before,
The other propping her white brow and throwing
Its ringlets out, under the skylight glowing.
So sat she fixed, and so observed was she
Of one, who at the door stood tenderly,—
Paulo,—who from a window seeing her
Go strait across the lawn, and guessing where,

Had thought she was in tears, and found, that day,
His usual efforts vain to keep away.
"May I come in?" said he:—it made her start,—
That smiling voice;—she coloured, pressed her
    heart
A moment, as for breath, and then with free
And usual tone said, "O yes,——certainly."
There's apt to be, at conscious times like these,
An affection of a bright-eyed ease,
An air of something quite serene and sure,
As if to seem so, was to be, secure.
With this the lovers met; with this they spoke,
With this they sat down to the self-same book,
And Paulo, by degrees, gently embraced
With one permitted arm her lovely waist;
And both their cheeks, like peaches on a tree,
Leaned with a touch together, thrillingly,
And o'er the book they hung, and nothing said,
And every lingering page grew longer as they read.

As thus they sat, and felt with leaps of heart
Their colour change, they came upon the part
Where fond Geneura, with her flame long nurst,
Smiled upon Launcelot, when he kissed her first:—
That touch, at last, through every fibre slid;
And Paulo turned, scarce knowing what he did,
Only he felt he could no more dissemble,
And kissed her, mouth to mouth, all in a tremble.
Sad were those hearts, and sweet was that long
    kiss:
Sacred be love from sight; whate'er it is.
The world was all forgot; the struggle o'er,
Desperate the joy.—That day they read no more.

CANTO IV.

HOW THE BRIDE RETURNED TO RAVENNA.

IT has surprised me often, as I write,
That I, who have of late known small delight,
Should thus pursue a mournful theme, and make
My very solace of distress partake;
And I have longed sometimes, I must confess,
To start at once from notes of wretchedness,
And in a key would make you rise and dance,
Strike up a blithe defiance to mischance.
But work begun, an interest in it, shame
At turning coward to the thoughts I frame,
Necessity to keep firm face on sorrow,
Some flattering, sweet-lipped question every
     morrow,
And above all, the poet's task divine
Of making tears themselves look up and shine,
And turning to a charm the sorrow past,
Have held me on, and shall do to the last.

Sorrow, to him who has a true touched ear,
Is but the discord of a warbling sphere,
A lurking contrast, which though harsh it be,
Distils the next note more deliciously.
E'en tales like this, founded on real woe,
From bitter seed to balmy fruitage grow:
The woe was earthly, fugitive, is past;
The song that sweetens it, may always last.
And even they, whose shattered hearts and frames
Make them unhappiest of poetic names,

What are they, if they know their calling high,
But crushed perfumes, exhaling to the sky?
Or weeping clouds, that but a while are seen,
Yet keep the earth they haste to, bright and
　　green?

Once, and but once,—nor with a scornful face
Tried worth will hear,—that scene again took
　　place.
Partly by chance they met, partly to see
The spot where they had last gone smilingly,
But most, from failure of all self-support ;—
And oh ! the meeting in that loved resort !
No peevishness there was, no loud distress,
No mean, recriminating selfishness ;
But a mute gush of hiding tears from one
Clasped to the core of him, who yet shed none,—
And self-accusings then, which he began,
And into which her tearful sweetness ran ;
And then kind looks, with meeting eyes again,
Starting to deprecate the other's pain ;
Till half persuasions they could scarce do wrong,
And sudden sense of wretchedness, more strong,
And—why should I add more?—again they parted,
He doubly torn for her, and she nigh broken-
　　hearted.

She never ventured in that spot again ;
And Paulo knew it, but could not refrain ;
He went again one day; and how it looked
The calm old shade !—His presence felt rebuked.
It seemed as if the hopes of his young heart,
His kindness, and his generous scorn of art,

Had all been a mere dream, or at the best
A vain negation that could stand no test,
And that on waking from his idle fit,
He found himself (how could he think of it !)
A selfish boaster, and a hypocrite.

That thought before had grieved him, but the
        pain
Cut sharp and sudden, now it came again.
Sick thoughts of late had made his body sick,
And this, in turn, to them grown strangely quick;
And pale he stood, and seemed to burst all o'er
Into moist anguish never felt before,
And with a dreadful certainty to know
His peace was gone, and all to come was woe ;
Francesca too,—the being made to bless,
Destined by him to the same wretchedness,—
It seemed as if such whelming thoughts must find
Some props for them, or he should lose his mind :
And find he did, not what the worse disease
Of want of charity calls sophistries,—
Nor what can cure a generous heart of pain,—
But humble guesses, helping to sustain.
He thought, with quick philosophy, of things,
Rarely found out except through sufferings,—
Of habit, circumstance, design, degree,
Merit, and will, and thoughtful charity ;
And these, although they pushed down, as they
        rose,
His self-respect, and all those morning shows
Of true and perfect, which his youth had built,
Pushed with them too the worst of others' guilt ;
And furnished him at least, with something kind,

On which to lean a sad and startled mind :
Till youth, and natural vigour, and the dread
Of self-betrayal, and a thought that spread
From time to time in gladness o'er his face,
That she he loved could have done nothing base,
Helped to restore him to his usual life,
Though grave at heart and with himself at strife ;
And he would rise betimes, day after day,
And mount his favourite horse, and ride away,
Miles in the country looking round about,
As he glode by, to force his thoughts without ;
And, when he found it vain, would pierce the
    shade
Of some enwooded field or closer glade,
And there dismounting, idly sit, and sigh,
Or pluck the grass beside him with vague eye,
And almost envy the poor beast, that went
Cropping it, here and there, with dumb content.
But thus, at least, he exercised his blood,
And kept it livelier than inaction could ;
And thus he earned for his thought-working head
The power of sleeping when he went to bed,
And was enabled still to wear away
That task of loaded hearts, another day.

But she, the gentler frame,—the shaken flower,—
Plucked up to wither in a foreign bower,—
The struggling, virtue-loving, fallen she,
The wife that was, the mother that might be,—
What could she do, unable thus to keep
Her strength alive, but sit, and think, and weep,
Forever stooping o'er her broidery frame,
Half blind, and longing till the night-time came,

When worn and wearied out with the day's sorrow
She might be still and senseless till the morrow !

And oh, the morrow, how it used to rise !
How would she open her despairing eyes,
And from the sense of the long lingering day
Rushing upon her, almost turn away,
Loathing the light, and groan to sleep again !
Then sighing once for all, to meet the pain,
She would get up in haste, and try to pass
The time in patience, wretched as it was ;
Till patience self, in her distempered sight,
Would seem a charm to which she had no right,
And trembling at the lip, and pale with fears,
She shook her head, and burst into fresh tears.
Old comforts now were not at her command :
The falcon reached in vain from off his stand ;
The flowers were not refreshed ; the very light,
The sunshine, seemed as if it shone at night ;
The least noise smote her like a sudden wound ;
And did she hear but the remotest sound
Of song or instrument about the place,
She hid with both her hands her streaming face.
But worse to her than all (and oh ! thought she,
That ever, ever, such a worse should be !)
The sight of infant was, or child at play ;
Then would she turn, and move her lips, and pray,
That Heaven would take her, if it pleased, away.

I pass the meetings Paulo had with her :—
Calm were they in their outward character,
Or pallid efforts, rather, to suppress
The pangs within, that either's might be less ;

And ended mostly with a passionate start
Of tears and kindness, when they came to part.
Thinner he grew, she thought, and pale with care;
"And I, 'twas I, that dashed his noble air !"
He saw her wasting, yet with placid show ;
And scarce could help exclaiming in his woe,
"O gentle creature, look not on me so."

But Prince Giovanni, whom her wan distress
Had touched, of late, with a new tenderness,
Which, to his fresh surprise, did but appear
To wound her more than when he was severe,
Began, with other helps, perhaps, to see
Strange things, and missed his brother's company.
What a convulsion was the first sensation !
Rage, wonder, misery, scorn, humiliation,
A self-love, struck as with a personal blow,
Gloomy revenge, a prospect full of woe,
All rushed upon him, like the sudden view
Of some new world, foreign to all he knew,
Where he had waked and found disease's visions
    true.

If any lingering hope that he was wrong
Smoothed o'er him now and then, 'twas not so long.
Next night, as sullenly awake he lay,
Considering what to do the approaching day ;
He heard his wife say something in her sleep :—
He shook, and listened ;—she began to weep,
And moaning loudlier, seemed to shake her head,
Till all at once articulate, she said,
"He loves his brother yet.—Dear Heaven, 'twas
    I—"
Then lower voiced—"Only—*do* let me die."

The prince looked at her hastily;—no more;
He dresses, takes his sword, and through the
  door
Goes, like a spirit, in the morning air ;—
His squire awaked attends ; and they repair,
Silent as wonder, to his brother's room :—
His squire calls him up too ; and forth they come.

The brothers meet,—Giovanni scarce in breath,
Yet firm and fierce, Paulo as pale as death.
"May I request, sir," said the prince, and frowned,
"Your ear a moment in the tilting ground."
"*There*, brother," answered Paulo, with an air
Surprised and shocked. "Yes, *brother*," cried he,
  "there."
The word smote crushingly ; and paler still,
He bowed, and moved his lips, as waiting on his
  will.

Giovanni turned, and from the tower descending,
The squires, with looks of sad surprise, attending,
They issued forth in the moist-striking air,
And toward the tilt-yard crossed a planted square.
 'Twas a fresh autumn dawn, vigorous and chill ;
The lightsome morning star was sparkling still,
Ere it turned in to heaven ; and far away
Appeared the streaky fingers of the day;
An opening in the trees took Paulo's eye,
As, with his brother, mutely he went by :
It was a glimpse of the tall wooded mound
That screen'd Francesca's favourite spot of ground :
Massy and dark in the clear twilight stood,
As in a lingering sleep, the solemn wood ;

And through the bowering arch, which led inside,
He almost fancied once, that he descried
A marble gleam, where the pavilion lay ;—
Starting he turned, and looked another way.

Arrived, and the two squires withdrawn apart,
The prince spoke low, as with a labouring heart,
And said, "Before you answer what you can,
I wish to tell you, as a gentleman,
That what you may confess" (and as he spoke
His voice with breathless and pale passion broke),
Will implicate no person known to you,
More than disquiet in its sleep may do,"
Paulo's heart bled ; he waved his hands, and bent
His head a little in acknowledgment ;
"Say then, sir, if you can," continued he,
"One word will do—you have not injured me :
Tell me but so, and I shall bear the pain
Of having asked a question I disdain ;—
But utter nothing, if not that one word ;
And meet me thus :"—he stopped, and drew his
    sword.

Paulo seemed firmer grown from his despair ;
He drew a little back ; and with the air
Of one who would do well, not from a right
To be well thought of, but in guilt's despite,
"I am," said he, "I know,—'twas not so ever—
But fight for it and with a brother.   Never."

"How !" with uplifted voice, exclaimed the
    other ;
"The vile pretence ! who asked you with a *brother?*
    II.   E

Brother ? O traitor to the noble name
Of Malatesta, I deny the claim.
What ! wound it deepest ? strike me to the core,
Me, and the hopes which I can have no more,
And then, as never Malatesta could,
Shrink from the letting a few drops of blood ? "

" It is not so," cried Paulo, " 'tis not so ;
But I would save you from a further woe."

" A further woe, recreant !" retorted he :
" I know of none : yes, one there still may be !
Save me the woe, save me the dire disgrace,
Of seeing one of an illustrious race
Bearing about a heart, which feared no law,
And a vile sword, which yet he dared not draw."

"Brother, dear brother !" Paulo cried, "nay,
        nay.
I'll use the word no more ;—but *peace*, I pray !
You trample on a soul, sunk at your feet !"
" 'Tis false !" exclaimed the prince; " 'tis a
        retreat
To which you fly, when manly wrongs pursue,
And fear the grave you bring a woman to."

A sudden start, yet not of pride or pain,
Paulo here gave ; he seemed to rise again,
And taking off his cap without a word,
He drew, and kissed the crossed hilt of his sword,
Looking to heaven ;—then, with a steady brow,
Mild, yet not feeble, said, " I'm ready now."

" A noble word !" exclaimed the prince, and
        smote

Preparingly on earth his firming foot :—
The squires rushed in between, in their despair,
But both the princes tell them to beware.

"Back, Gerard," cries Giovanni; "I require
No teacher here, but an observant squire."
"Back, Tristan," Paulo cries; "fear not for me;
All is not worst that so appears to thee. ˆ

And here," said he, "a word." The poor
    youth came,
Starting in sweeter tears to hear his name :
A whisper, and a charge there seemed to be,
Given to him kindly yet inflexibly :
Both squires then drew apart again, and stood
Mournfully both, each in his several mood,—
The one half sullen at these dreadful freaks,
The other with the tears streaming down both his
    cheeks.

The prince attacked with all his might and main,
Nor seemed the other slow to strike again ;
Yet as the fight grew warm, 'twas evident,
One fought to wound, the other to prevent :
Giovanni pressed, and pushed, and shifted aim,
And played his weapon like a tongue of flame ;
Paulo retired, and warded, turned on heel,
And led him, step by step, round like a wheel.
Sometimes indeed he feigned an angrier start,
But still relapsed, and played his former part.
  "What !" cried Giovanni, who grew still more
    fierce,
"Fighting in sport? Playing your cart and tierce?"

"Not so, my prince," said Paulo; "have a care
How you think so, or I shall wound you there."
He stamped, and watching as he spoke the word,
Drove, with his breast, full on his brother's sword.

  'Twas done. He staggered; and in falling prest
Giovanni's foot with his right hand and breast:
Then on his elbow turned, and raising t'other,
He smiled and said, "No fault of yours, my
      brother;
An accident—a slip—the finishing one
To errors by that poor old man begun.
You'll not—you'll not"—his heart leaped on before,
And choked his utterance; but he smiled once
      more,
For as his hand grew lax, he felt it prest;—
And so, his dim eyes sliding into rest,
He turned him round, and dropt with hiding head,
And in that loosening drop his spirit fled.

  But noble passion touched Giovanni's soul;
He seemed to feel the clouds of habit roll
Away from him at once, with all their scorning,
And out he spoke, in the clear air of morning:—
  "By heaven, by heaven, and all the better part
Of us poor creatures with a human heart,
I trust we reap at last, as well as plough;—
But there, meantime, my brother, liest thou:
And, Paulo, thou wert the completest knight,
That ever rode with banner to the fight;
And thou wert the most beautiful to see,
That ever came in press of chivalry;
And of a sinful man, thou wert the best,
That ever for his friend put spear in rest;

And thou wert the most meek and cordial,
That ever among ladies eat in hall ;
And thou wert still, for all that bosom gored,
The kindest man that ever struck with sword."

At this the words forsook his tongue ; and he,
Who scarcely had shed tears since infancy,
Felt his stern visage thrill, and meekly bowed
His head, and for his brother wept aloud.
 The squires with glimmering tears —Tristan,
  indeed,
Heart-struck, and hardly able to proceed,—
Double their scarfs about the fatal wound,
And raise the body up to quit the ground.
Giovanni starts ; and motioning to take
The way they came, follows his brother back,
And having seen him laid upon the bed,
No further look he gave him, nor tear shed,
But went away, such as he used to be,
With looks of stately will and calm austerity.

 Tristan, who when he was to make the best
Of something sad and not to be redressed,
Could show a heart as firm as it was kind,
Now locked his tears up, and seemed all resigned,
And to Francesca's chamber took his way,
To tell her what his master bade him say.
He found her ladies up and down the stairs,
Moving with noiseless caution, and in tears,
And that the sad news had before him got,
Though she herself, it seemed, yet knew it not.
The door, as tenderly as miser's purse,
Was opened to him by her aged nurse,

Who shaking her old head, and pressing close
Her withered lips to keep the tears that rose,
Made signs she guessed what 'twas he came about,
And so his arm squeezed gently, and went out.

The princess, who had passed a fearful night,
Toiling with dreams,—fright crowding upon fright,
Had missed her husband at that early hour, ˙
And when she tried to rise found she'd no power.
Yet as her body seemed to go, her mind
Felt, though in anguish still, strangely resigned ;
And moving not, nor weeping, mute she lay,
Wasting in patient gravity away.
The nurse, sometime before, with gentle creep
Had drawn the curtains, hoping she might sleep :
But suddenly she asked, though not with fear,
" Brangin, what bustle's that I seem to hear ? "
And the poor creature who the news had heard,
Pretending to be busy, had just stirred
Something about the room, and answered not a
　　word.

　　" Who's there ? " said that sweet voice, kindly
　　　　and clear,
Which in its stronger days was joy to hear :—
Its weakness now almost deprived the squire
Of his new firmness, but approaching nigher,
" Madam," said he, " 'tis I ; one who may say,.
He loves his friends more than himself to-day ;—
Tristan."—She paused a little, and then said—
" Tristan, my friend, what noise thus haunts my
　　　　head ?
Something I'm sure has happened—tell me what—
I can bear all, though you may fancy not."

"Madam," replied the squire, "you are, I know,
All sweetness—pardon me for saying so.
My master bade me say then," resumed he,
"That he spoke firmly when he told it me,—
That I was, also, madam, to your ear
Firmly to speak, and you firmly to hear,—
That he was forced this day, whether or no,
To combat with the prince ; and that although
His noble brother was no fratricide,
Yet in that fight, and on his sword,—he died."

"I understand," with firmness answered she,
More low in voice, but still composedly.
"Now, Tristan—faithful friend—leave me ; and
  take
This trifle here, and keep it for my sake."
So saying, from the curtains she put forth
Her thin white hand, that held a ring of worth;
And he, with tears no longer to be kept
From quenching his heart's thirst, silently wept,
And kneeling, took the ring, and touched her
  hand
To either streaming eye, with homage bland,
And looking on it once, gently up started,
And in his reverent stillness, so departed.

Her favourite lady then with the old nurse
Returned, and fearing she must now be worse,
Gently withdrew the curtains, and look'd in :—
O, who that feels one godlike spark within,
Shall say that earthly suffering cancels not frail
  sin ?
There lay she praying, upwardly intent,
Like a fair statue on a monument,

With her two trembling hands together prest,
Palm against palm, and pointing from her breast,
She ceased ; and turning slowly tow'rds the wall,
They saw her tremble sharply, feet and all,—
Then suddenly be still.   Near and more near
They bent with pale inquiry and close ear;
Her eyes were shut—no motion—not a breath—
The gentle sufferer was at peace in death.

I pass the grief that struck to every face,
And the mute anguish all about that place,
In which the silent people, here and there,
Went soft, as if she still could feel their care.
The gentle-tempered for a while forgot
Their own distress, or wept the common lot :
The warmer, apter now to take offence,
Yet hushed as they rebuked, and wondered
          whence
Others at such a time could get their want of
          sense.

Fain would I haste, indeed, to finish all;
And so at once I reach the funeral.
Private 'twas fancied it must be, though some
Thought that her sire, the poor old duke, would
          come :
And some were wondering in their pity, whether.
The lovers might not have one grave together.

Next day, however, from the palace-gate,
A blast of trumpets blew, like voice of fate,
And all in sable clad forth came again
Of knights and squires the former sprightly train,

Gerard was next, and then a rank of friars ;
And then, with heralds on each side, two squires,
The one of whom upon a cushion bore
The coroneted helm Prince Paulo wore,
His shield the other ;—then there was a space,
And in the middle, with a doubtful pace,
His horse succeeded, plumed and trapped in black,
Bearing the sword and banner on his back :
The noble creature, as in state he trod,
Appeared as if he missed his princely load ;
And with back-rolling eye and lingering pride,
To hope his master still might come to ride.
Then Tristan, heedless of what passed around,
Rode by himself, with eyes upon the ground.
Then heralds in a row : and last of all
Appeared a hearse, hung with an ermined pall,
And bearing on its top, together set,
A prince's and princess's coronet.
Mutely they issued forth, black, slow, dejected,
Nor stopped within the walls, as most expected,
But passed the gates—the bridge—the last abode—
And towards Ravenna held their silent road.

The prince, it seems, struck since his brother's
          death,
With what he hinted at his dying breath,
And told by others now of all they knew,
Had instantly determined what to do ;
And from a mingled feeling, which he strove
To hide no longer from his taught self-love,
Of sorrow, shame, resentment, and a sense
Of justice owing to that first offence,
Had, on the day preceding, written word

To the old Duke of all that had occurred :
" And though I shall not " (so concluded he),
" Otherwise touch thine age's misery,
Yet as I would that both one grave should hide,
Which can, and must not be, where I reside,
'Tis fit, though all have something to deplore,
That he who joined them once, should keep to part
      no more."

   The wretched father, who, when he had read
This letter, felt it wither his grey head,
And ever since had paced his room about,
Trembling, and at the windows looking out,
Had given such orders as he well could frame
To meet devoutly whatsoever came ;
And, as the news immediately took flight,
Few in Ravenna went to sleep that night,
But talked the business over, and reviewed
All that they knew of her, the fair and good ;
And so with wondering sorrow, the next day,
Waited till they should see that sad array.

   The days were then at close of autumn,—still,
A little rainy, and towards nightfall chill ;
There was a fitful moaning air abroad ;
And ever and anon, over the road,
The last few leaves came fluttering from the trees,
Whose trunks now thronged to sight, in dark
      varieties.
The people, who, from reverence, kept at home,
Listened till after noon to hear them come ;
And hour on hour went by, and nought was heard
But some chance horseman, or the wind that
      stirred,

Till towards the vesper hour; and then, 'twas said,
Some heard a voice, which seemed as if it read;
And others said, that they could hear a sound
Of many horses trampling the moist ground.
Still nothing came :—till on a sudden, just
As the wind opened in a rising gust,
A voice of chaunting rose, and, as it spread,
They plainly heard the anthem for the dead.
It was the choristers who went to meet
The train, and now were entering the first street.
Then turned aside that city, young and old,
And in their lifted hands the gushing sorrow
   rolled.

But of the older people few could bear
To keep the window, when the train drew near;
And all felt double tenderness to see
The bier approaching, slow and steadily,
On which those two in senseless coldness lay,
Who but a few short months—it seem'd a day,
Had left their walls, lovely in form and mind;
In sunny manhood he,—she first of womankind.

They say that when Duke Guido saw them come
He clasped his hands, and looking round the room,
Lost his old wits for ever. From the morrow
None saw him after. But no more of sorrow.

On that same night, those lovers silently
Were buried in one grave, under a tree.
There, side by side, and hand in hand, they lay
In the green ground ;—and on fine nights in May
Young hearts betrothed used to go there to pray.

THE PANTHER.[1]

["Hero and Leander," 1819. "Works," 1832, 1844, 1857, 1860. "Rimini," &c., 1844. Kent, 1889. "Canterbury Poets," 1889.]

THE panther leaped to the front of his
　　　lair,
　　And stood with a foot up, and snuffed
　　　the air ;
He quivered his tongue from his panting mouth,
And looked with a yearning towards the south ;
For he scented afar in the coming breeze
News of the gums and their blossoming trees ;
And out of Armenia that same day
He and his race came bounding away.
Over the mountains and down to the plains
Like Bacchus's panthers with wine in their veins,
They came where the woods wept odorous rains ;
And there, with a quivering, every beast
Fell to his old Pamphylian feast.

　The people who lived not far away,
Heard the roaring on that same day ;
And they said, as they lay in their carpeted rooms,
"The panthers are come, and are drinking the
　　　gums ; "
And some of them going with swords and spears
To gather their share of the rich round tears,

---

[1] The circumstances of this poem are taken from Philostratus' "Life of Apollonius of Tyæna." (Advertisement to "Hero and Leander, &c.")

The panther I spoke of followed them back ;
And dumbly they let him tread close in the track,
And lured him after them into the town ;
And then they let the portcullis down,
And took the panther, which happened to be
The largest was seen in all Pamphily.

By every one there was the panther admired,
So fine was his shape and so sleekly attired,
And such an air, both princely and swift,
He had, when giving a sudden lift
To his mighty paw, he'd turn at a sound, ⎫
And so stand panting and looking around, ⎬
As if he attended a monarch crowned. ⎭
And truly, they wondered the more to behold
About his neck a collar of gold,
On which was written, in characters broad,
" Arsaces the king to the Nysian God."
So they tied to the collar a golden chain,
Which made the panther a captive again,
And by degrees he grew fearful and still,
As if he had lost his lordly will.

But now came the spring, when free-born love
Calls up nature in forest and grove,
And makes each thing leap forth, and be
Loving, and lovely, and blithe as he.
The panther he felt the thrill of the air,
And he gave a leap up, like that at his lair ;
He felt the sharp sweetness more strengthen his ⎫
    veins ⎪
Ten times than ever the spicy rains, ⎬
And ere they're aware, he has burst his chains: ⎭

He has burst his chains, and ah, ha ! he's gone,⎫
And the links and the gazers are left alone,　⎬
And off to the mountains the panther's flown.　⎭

Now what made the panther a prisoner be ?
Lo ! 'twas the spices and luxury.
And what set that lordly panther free ?
'Twas Love !—'twas Love !—'twas no one but he.

MAHMOUD.[1]

["Liberal," No. IV., 1823. "Works," 1832, 1844, 1857, 1860. Kent, 1889. "Canterbury Poets," 1889.]

TO RICHARD HENRY HORNE.[2]

Horne, hear a theme that should have had its dues
From thine own passionate and thoughtful Muse.

I HAVE just read a most amazing thing,
A true and noble story of a king :
And to show all men, by these presents, how
Good kings can please a Liberal, even now
I'll vent the warmth it gave me in a verse :
But recollect—these kings and emperors
Are very scarce ; and when they do appear,
Had better not have graced that drunken sphere,
Which hurts the few whose brains can bear it best,

[1] This is Mahmoud the Garnevide, whose history has been told by Gibbon.
[2] The dedication was introduced when the poem was reprinted in the 1844 edition of the "Poetical Works."

And turns the unhappy heads of all the rest.
This prince was worthy to have ruled a state
Plain as his heart, and by its freedom great :
But stripped of their gilt stuff, at what would
      t'others rate?

There came a man, making his hasty moan
Before the Sultan Mahmoud on his throne,
And crying out—"My sorrow is my right,
And I *will* see the Sultan, and to-night."
" Sorrow," said Mahmoud, " is a reverend thing:
I recognize its right, as king with king ;
Speak on." "A fiend has got into my house,"
Exclaimed the staring man, "and tortures us :
One of thine officers ;—he comes, the abhorred,
And takes possession of my house, my board,
My bed :—I have two daughters and a wife,
And the wild villain comes, and makes me mad
      with life."

"Is he there now ?" said Mahmoud :—"No ;
      he left
The house when I did, of my wits bereft ;
And laughed me down the street, because I vowed
I'd bring the prince himself to lay him in his shroud,
I'm mad with want, I'm mad with misery,
And oh, thou Sultan Mahmoud, God cries out for
      thee !" .

The Sultan comforted the man, and said,
" Go home, and I will send thee wine and bread,"
(For he was poor), "and other comforts. Go ;
And should the wretch return, let Sultan Mahmoud
      know."

In two days' time, with haggard eyes and beard,
And shaken voice, the suitor reappeared,
And said, " He's come."—Mahmoud said not a
    word,
But rose and took four slaves, each with a sword,
And went with the vexed man. They reach the
    place,
And hear a voice, and see a female face,
That to the window fluttered in affright.
" Go in," said Mahmoud, "and put out the light;
But tell the females first to leave the room ;
And when the drunkard follows them, we come."

The man went in.   There was a cry, and hark !
A table falls, the window is struck dark ;
Forth rush the breathless women ; and behind
With curses comes the fiend in desperate mind.
In vain : the sabres soon cut short the strife,
And chop the shrieking wretch, and drink his
    bloody life.

"Now *light* the light," the Sultan cried aloud.
'Twas done, he took it in his hand, and bowed
Over the corpse, and looked upon the face ;
Then turned and knelt beside it in the place,
And said a prayer, and from his lips there crept
Some gentle words of pleasure, and he wept.
In reverent silence the spectators wait,
Then bring him at his call both wine and meat ;
And when he had refreshed his noble heart,
He bade his host be blest, and rose up to depart.

The man amazed, all mildness now, and tears,
Fell at the Sultan's feet, with many prayers,

And begged him to vouchsafe to tell his slave,
The reason first of that command he gave
About the light ; then when he saw the face,
Why he knelt down ; and lastly, how it was,
That fare so poor as his detained him in the place.

The Sultan said, with much humanity,
" Since first I saw thee come, and heard thy cry,
I could not rid me of a dread, that one
By whom such daring villanies were done,
Must be some lord of mine, perhaps a lawless son.
Whoe'er he was, I knew my task, but feared
A father's heart, in case the worst appeared.
For this I had the light put out ; but when
I saw the face, and found a stranger slain,
I knelt and thanked the sovereign arbiter,
Whose work I had performed through pain and fear ;
And then I rose, and was refreshed with food,
The first time since thou cam'st, and marr'dst my
　　　solitude."

THE GLOVE AND THE LIONS.[1]

["New Monthly Magazine," May, 1836. "Works,"
1844, 1857, 1860. "Rimini," &c., 1844. Kent, 1889.]

ING FRANCIS was a hearty king, and
　　　loved a royal sport,
　　　And one day as his lions fought, sat
　　　looking on the court ;
The nobles filled the benches, with the ladies by
　　　their side,

---

[1] See the story in St. Felix's "History of Paris," who
quoted it from Brantome.

And 'mongst them sat the Count de Lorge, with
    one for whom he sighed :
And truly 'twas a gallant thing to see that crowning
    show,
Valour and love, and a king above, and the royal
    beasts below.

Ramped and roared the lions, with horrid laughing
    jaws ;
They bit, they glared, gave blows like bears, a
    wind went with their paws ;
With wallowing might and stifled roar they rolled
    on one another,
Till all the pit with sand and mane, was in a
    thunderous smother ;
The bloody foam above the bars came whizzing
    through the air ;
Said Francis then, " Faith, gentlemen, we're
    better here than there."

De Lorge's love o'erheard the King, a beauteous
    lively dame,
With smiling lips and sharp bright eyes, which
    always seemed the same ;
She thought, the Count my lover is brave as
    brave can be ;
He surely would do wondrous things to show his
    love of me ;
King, ladies, lovers, all look on ; the occasion is
    divine ;
I'll drop my glove, to prove his love ; great glory
    will be mine.

She dropped her glove, to prove his love, then
    looked at him and smiled ;
He bowed, and in a moment leaped among the
    lions wild :
The leap was quick, return was quick, he has re-
    gained his place,
Then threw the glove, but not with love, right in
    the lady's face.
" By Heav'n ! " said Francis, " rightly done ! "
    and he rose from where he sat :
" No love," quoth he, " but vanity, sets love a
    task like that."

ABOU BEN ADHEM.[1]

["Rimini," &c., 1844. "Works," 1844, 1857, 1860.
"Favourite Poems," 1877. Kent, 1889. "Canterbury
Poets," 1889.]

ABOU BEN ADHEM (may his tribe
    increase !)
Awoke one night from a deep dream of
    peace,
And saw, within the moonlight in his room,
Making it rich, and like a lily in bloom,

[1] "On rapporte de lui (Abou-Ishak-Ben-Adhem), qu'il
vit en songe un ange qui écrivoit, et que lui ayant demandé
ce qu'il faisoit, cet ange lui répondit : ' J'écris le nom de
ceux qui aiment sincèrement Dieu, tels que sont Malek-Ben-
Dinar, Thaber-al-Benani, Aioud-al-Sakhtiani, &c.' Alors
il dit à l'ange, ' Ne suis-je point parmi ces gens-là ? '—' Non,'
lui répondit l'ange. ' Hé bien,' répliqua-t-il, ' écrivez-moi,
je vous prie, pour l'amour d'eux, en qualité d'ami de ceux
qui aiment Dieu.' L'on ajoute, que le même ange lui révéla

An angel writing in a book of gold :—
Exceeding peace had made Ben Adhem bold,
And to the presence in the room he said,
"What writest thou?"—The vision raised its head,
And with a look made of all sweet accord,
Answered, "The names of those who love the
  Lord."
"And is mine one?" said Abou. "Nay, not so,"
Replied the angel. Abou spoke more low,
But cheerly still ; and said, "I pray thee then,
Write me as one that loves his fellow-men."

The angel wrote, and vanished. The next night
It came again with a great wakening light,
And showed the names whom love of God had
  blessed,
And lo! Ben Adhem's name led all the rest.

THE FANCY CONCERT.

["Ainsworth's Magazine," vol. vii., 1845. "A Gallery of
Illustrious Characters," by late Daniel Maclise, R.A., 1873.
"Poetical Works," Boston, 1857.]

THEY talked of their concerts, and
  singers, and scores,
  And pitied the fever that kept me in-
  doors ;
And I smiled in my thought, and said, "O ye
 sweet fancies,

bientôt après, qu'il avoit reçu ordre de Dieu de le mettre à
la tête de tous les autres."—D'HERBELOT, *Bibliothèque
Orientale* (1781). Tom. i. p. 161, in voc. *Adhem.*

And animal spirits, that still in your dances
Come bringing me visions to comfort my care,
Now fetch me a concert—imparadise air." [1]

Then a wind like a storm out of Eden, came
    pouring
Fierce into my room, and made tremble the floor-
    ing;
And filled with a sudden impetuous trample
Of heaven, its corners; and swelled it to ample
Dimensions to breathe in, and space for all power;
Which falling as suddenly, lo ! the sweet flower
Of an exquisite fairy-voice opened its blessing ;
And ever and aye, to its constant addressing,
There came, falling in with it, each in the last,
Flageolets one by one, and flutes blowing more
    fast,
And hautboys and clarinets, acrid of reed,
And the violin, smoothlier sustaining the speed
As the rich tempest gathered, and busy-ringing
    moons
Of tambours, and huge basses, and giant bassoons;
And the golden trombone,—that darteth its tongue
Like a bee of the gods ; nor was absent the
    gong,
Like a sudden, fate-bringing, oracular sound,
Of earth's iron genius, burst up from the ground,
A terrible slave, come to wait on his masters
The gods, with exultings that clang like disasters ;
And then spoke the organs, the very gods they,
Like thunders that roll on a wind-blowing day ;

---

[1] " Imparadised in one another's arms."—Milton. The
word is of Italian origin.

And taking the rule of the roar in their hands,
Lo, the Genii of Music came out of all lands ;
And one of them said, "Will my lord tell his
    slave,
What concert 'twould please his Firesideship to
    have ?"

Then I said, in a tone of immense will and plea-
    sure,
" Let orchestras rise to some exquisite measure ;
And let there be lights and be odours ; and let
The lovers of music serenely be set ;
And then with their singers in lily-white stoles,
And themselves clad in rose-colour, fetch me the
    souls
Of all the composers accounted divinest,
And, with their own hands, let them play me their
    finest."

And lo ! was performed my immense will and
    pleasure,
And orchestras rose to an exquisite measure ;
And lights were about me, and odours, and set
Were the lovers of music all wondrously met ;
And then, with their singers in lily-white stoles,
And themselves clad in rose-colour, in came the
    souls
Of all the composers accounted divinest,
And, with their own hands, did they play me their
    finest.

Oh, truly, was Italy heard then, and Germany,
Melody's heart, and the rich brain of harmony ;

Pure Paisiello, whose airs are as new
Though we know them by heart, as may-blossoms
      and dew ;
And Nature's twin son, Pergolesi ; and Bach,
Old father of fugues, with his endless fine talk ;
And Gluck,[1] who saw gods ; and the learned sweet
      feeling
Of Haydn ; and Winter, whose sorrows are healing ;
And gentlest Corelli, whose bowing seems made
For a hand with a jewel ; and Handel arrayed
In Olympian thunders, vast lord of the spheres,
Yet pious himself, with his blindness in tears,
A lover withal, and a conqueror, whose marches
Bring demi-gods under victorious arches ;
Then Arne,[2] sweet and tricksome ; and masterly
      Purcell,
Lay-clerical soul ; and Mozart universal,
But chiefly with exquisite gallantries found,
With a grove in the distance of holier sound ;
Nor forgot was thy dulcitude, loving Sacchini ;
Nor love, young and dying, in shape of Bellini ;

---

[1] "I see gods ascending out of the earth."—*Vide* the passage of "Saul and the Witch of Endor," in the Bible. A sense of the god-like and supernatural always appears to me to attend the noble and affecting music of Gluck.

[2] It seems a fashion of late in musical quarters to undervalue Arne. His defects are obvious when contrasted with the natural recitative and unsought melodies of the great Italians, and with the rich instrumentation of Mozart and the modern operas ; but may it be permitted an unprofessional lover of music to think that there are few melodies more touchingly fluent than "Water Parted," and very few songs indeed more original, charming, and to the purpose, than his "Cuckoo Song," and "Where the Bee Sucks?"

Nor Weber, nor Himmel, nor mirth's sweetest
    name,
Cimarosa ; much less the great organ-voiced fame
Of Marcello, that hushed the Venetian sea ;
And strange was the shout, when it wept, hearing
    thee,
Thou soul full of grace as of grief, my heart-cloven,
My poor, my most rich, my all-feeling Beethoven.

O'er all, like a passion, great Pasta [1] was heard,
As high as her heart, that truth-uttering bird ;
And Banti was there ; and Grassini, that goddess !
Dark, deep-toned, large, lovely, with glorious
    bodice ;
And Mara ; and Malibran, stung to the tips
Of her fingers with pleasure ; and rich Fodor's lips ;
And manly in face as in tone, Angrisani ;
And Naldi, thy whim ; and thy grace, Tramezzani ;
And was it a voice, or what was it ? say,
That like a fallen angel beginning to pray,
Was the soul of all tears and celestial despair ?
Paganini it was, 'twixt his dark flowing hair.

So now we had instrument, now we had song :
Now chorus, a thousand-voiced, one-hearted throng;
Now pauses that pampered resumption, and now—
But who shall describe what was played us, or how?

---

[1] Pasta, who is not dead, is here killed for the occasion,
being the singer of the greatest genius it has ever been my
good fortune to hear. Her tones latterly failed her, and she
may have always had superiors in some other respects ; but
for power to move the heart and the imagination I never
witnessed her equal. The reason was, that possessing both
of the most genuine sort, she cared for nothing but truth.

'Twas wonder, 'twas transport, humility, pride ;
'Twas the heart of the mistress that sat by one's
    side ;
'Twas the graces invisible moulding the air
Into all that is shapely, and lovely, and fair,
And running our fancies their tenderest rounds
Of endearments and luxuries, turned into sounds,
'Twas argument even, the logic of tones ;
'Twas memory, 'twas wishes, 'twas laughter, 'twas
    moans ;
'Twas pity and love, in pure impulse obeyed ;
'Twas the breath of the stuff of which passion is
    made.

And these are the concerts I have at my will ;
Then dismiss them, and patiently think of your
    " bill."
(*Aside*) Yet Lablache, after all, makes me long
    to go, still.

THE ROYAL LINE.

["Companion," Feb. 6th, 1828. "Works," 1860. Kent,
1889.]

William I.	The sturdy Conq'ror, politic, severe ;
William II.	Light-minded Rufus, dying like the deer ;
Henry I.	Beau-clerc, who everything but virtue knew ;
Stephen.	Stephen, who graced the lawless sword he drew ;

Henry II.	Fine Henry, hapless in his sons and priest ;
Richard I.	Richard, the glorious trifler in the East ;
John.	John, the mean wretch, tyrant and slave, a liar ;
Henry III.	Imbecile Henry, worthy of his sire ;
Edward I.	Long-shanks, well named, a great encroacher he ;
Edward II.	Edward the minion dying dreadfully;
Edward III.	The splendid veteran, weak in his decline ;
Richard II.	Another minion, sure untimely sign ;
Henry IV.	Usurping Lancaster, whom wrongs advance ;
Henry V.	Harry the Fifth, the tennis-boy of France ;
Henry VI.	The beadsman, praying while his Margaret fought ;
Edward IV.	Edward, too sensual for a kindly thought ;
Edward V.	The little head, that never wore the crown ;
Richard III.	Crookback, to nature giving frown for frown ;
Henry VII.	Close-hearted Henry, the shrewd carking sire ;
Henry VIII.	The British Bluebeard, fat, and full of ire ;
Edward VI.	The sickly boy, endowing and endowed ;
Mary.	Ill Mary, lighting many a living shroud ;

Elizabeth.	The lion-queen, with her stiff muslin mane ;
James I.	The shambling pedant, and his minion train ;
Charles I.	Weak Charles, the victim of the dawn of right ;
Cromwell.	Cromwell, misuser of his home-spun might ;
Charles II.	The swarthy scapegrace, all for ease and wit ;
James II.	The bigot out of season, forced to quit ;
William III.	The Dutchman, called to see our vessel through ;
Anne.	Anna made great by Conquering Marlborough ;
George I.	George, vulgar soul, a woman-hated name ;
George II.	Another, fonder of his fee than fame ;
George III.	A third, too weak, instead of strong, to swerve ;
George IV.	And fourth, whom Canning and Sir Will preserve.

CORONATION SOLILOQUY

OF HIS MAJESTY KING GEORGE THE FOURTH.

1821.[1]

["Works," 1860.   Kent, 1889.]

To the tune of *Amo, amas,*
I love a lass
  As cedar tall and slender;
Sweet cowslip's grace,
. *Is her nominative case,*
  And she's of the feminine gender.
Horum quorum,
Sunt divorum,
  Harum, scarum, divo;
Tag rag, merry derry, periwig and hatband,
Hic, hoc, harum, genitivo.
O'KEEFE.

I.

EGO, regis,
  Good God, what's this?
    What, only half my Peeries!
Regas, regat,
  Good God, what's that?
    The voice is like my deary's!
Oh, no more there;
Shut the door there;
    Harum, scarum, strife O!
Bags, Bags, Sherry Derry, periwigs, and fat lads,
    Save us from our wife O!

[1] But from a revised and augmented copy, superseding the first imperfect sketch, and not published till 1860.

II.

I decline a
C. Regina,
   Rex alone's more handsome :
Oh what luck, Sir,
Exit uxor !
   Rursus ego a man *sum.*
Glory, glory !
How will story
   Tell how I was gazed at !
Perfect from my pumps, to the plumes above my
   hat-band,
   All are me amazed at !

III.

Yes, my hat, Sirs,
Think of that, Sirs,
   Vast, and plumed, and Spain-like :
See my big,
Grand robes ; my wig
   Young, yet lion-mane like.
Glory ! glory !
I'm not hoary ;
   Age it can't come o'er me :
Mad caps, grave caps, gazing on the grand man,
   All alike adore me.

IV.

I know where
A fat, a fair,
   Sweet other self is doting :
I'd reply

With wink of eye,
    But fear the newsman noting.
Hah ! the Toying,
Never cloying,
    Cometh to console me :
Crowns and sceptres, jewellery, state swords, —
    Who now shall control me ?

v.

Must I walk now !
What a baulk now !
    Non est regis talis.
O, for youth now !
For in truth now,
    Non sum eram qualis.
Well, well, roar us,
On before us,
    Harum, flarum, stout O,
Stately, greatly, periwig and trumpets, —
    Oh, could I leave but my gout O !

vi.

What a *dies !*
How it fri-es !
    Handkerchiefs for sixty.
Approbatio !
Sibilatio !
    How I feel betwixt ye !
Curlies, burlies,
Dukes and earlies,
    Bangs and clangs of band O !
Shouty, flouty, heavy rig, and gouty,
    When shall I come to a stand O !

VII.

Bliss at last !
The street is passed ;
    The aisle—I've dragged me through it:
Oh the rare
Old crowning chair !
    I fear I flopped into it.
Balmy, balmy,
Comes the psalmy ;
    Bland the organ blows me ;
Crown down coming on a periwig that fits me,
    All right royal shows me !

VIII.

Oh how *bona*
My *corona !*
    Sitting so how *dulcis !*
My *oculus* grim,
And my *sceptrum* slim,
    And proud, as I hold it, my pulse is !
Shout us, chorus ;
Organs, roar us ;
    Realms, let a secret start ye :—
Dragon-killing George on the coin is myself,
    And the dragon is Bonaparte.

IX.

And yet alas !
Must e'en *I* pass
    Through hisses again on foot, Sirs !
Oh pang profound !
And I now walk crowned,
    And with sceptre in hand to boot, Sirs !

I go, I go,
With a fire in my toe,
    I'm bowing, blasting, baking !
Hall, O Hall, ope your doors, and let your guest in ;
    Every inch I'm à—king.

X.

But now we dine !
Oh word divine,
    Beyond what e'en has crown'd it !
Envy may call
Great monarchs small,
    But feast, and you dumb-found it.
Brandy, brandy,
To steady me handy
    For playing my knife and fork, O !
Green fat, and devilry, shall warrant me ere bed-time,
    In drawing my twentieth cork O.

XI.

Hah, my Champy !
Plumy, trampy !
    Astley's best can't beat him !
See his frown !
His glove thrown down !
    Should a foe appear, he'd eat him !.
Glory, glory,
Glut and glory,—
I mean poury,
Glut and poury,—
Poury, mory,
Splash and floory,

Crown us, drown us, *vivo !*
Cram dram, never end, plethora be d—ned, man ;
Vivat Rex dead-alive O !

QUIET EVENINGS.[1]

TO T[HOMAS] B[ARNES], ESQ.

[" Examiner," Feb. 14th, 1813. " Feast of the Poets,"
1814, and 2nd ed., 1815. " Works," 1832, 1844, 1857, 1860.
" Book of Sonnets," 1867.]

EAR BARNES, whose native taste,
solid and clear,
The throng of life has strengthened
without harm,
You know the rural feeling, and the charm
That stillness has for a world-fretted ear :
'Tis now deep whispering all about me here
With thousand tiny hushings, like a swarm
Of atom bees, or fairies in alarm,
Or noise of numerous bliss from distant sphere.

This charm our evening hours duly restore,—
Nought heard through all our little, lull'd abode,
Save the crisp fire, or leaf of book turned o'er,
Or watch-dog, or the ring of frosty road.

[1] The reader will perceive, from the nature of the following lines, as well as from the date of them, that they were
very far from being written in the editor's present residence
[Horsemonger Lane Jail], which cannot exactly be described,
as a " little lull'd abode," and whose watch-dogs, though it
has enough of them, are not of a description to excite pleasant or pastoral associations.

Wants there no other sound, then?—yes, one
        more,—
    The voice of friendly visiting, long owed.

HAMPSTEAD, *Jan. 20th,* 1813.

I.

TO HAMPSTEAD.[1]

[" Examiner," Aug. 29th, 1813. " Feast of the Poets,"
2nd ed., 1815. " Works," 1860. " Canterbury Poets," 1889.]

SWEET upland, to whose walks, with
            fond repair,
            Out of thy western slope I took my
            rise
Day after day, and on these feverish eyes
Met the moist fingers of the bathing air ;—
If health, unearned of thee, I may not share,
    Keep it, I pray thee, where my memory lies,
    In thy green lanes, brown dells, and breezy
        skies,
Till I return, and find thee doubly fair.

Wait then my coming, on that lightsome land,
    Health, and the joy that out of nature springs,
        And Freedom's air-blown locks ;—but stay
            with me,
Friendship, frank entering with the cordial hand,
    And Honour, and the Muse with growing wings,
        And Love Domestic, smiling equably.

SURREY JAIL, *Aug. 27th,* 1813.

1 I have numbered the sonnets according to the text of
the "Examiner." Why III. and V. were omitted, and two
of them were numbered VII., I know not.—ED.

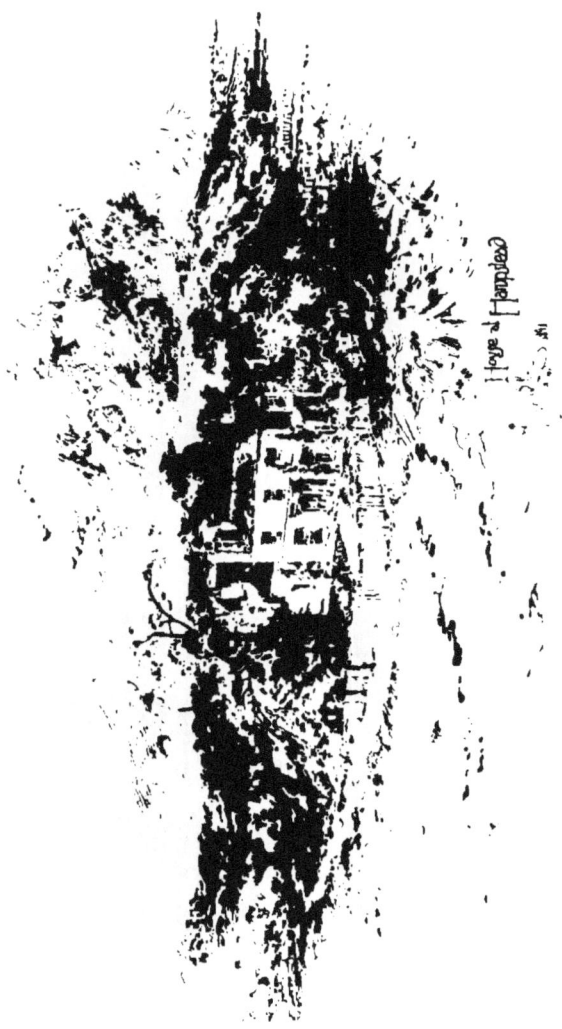

Hope of [Hampden]

II.

TO HAMPSTEAD.

["Examiner," Aug. 7th, 1814. "Feast of the Poets,"
2nd ed., 1815. "Works," 1860.]

THEY tell me, when my tongue grows
warm on thee,
Dear gentle hill, with tresses green
and bright,
That thou art wanting in the finishing sight
Sweetest of all for summer eyes to see;—
That whatsoe'er thy charm of tower and tree,
Of dell wrapped in, or airy-viewing height,
No water looks from out thy face with light,
Or waits upon thy walks refreshfully.

It may be so,—casual though pond or brook :—
Yet not to me so full of all that's fair.
Though fruit-embowered, with fingering sun
between,
Were the divinest fount in Fancy's nook,
In which the nymphs sit tying up their hair,
Their white backs glistening through the
myrtles green.

SURREY JAIL, *Aug.*, 1814.

IV.

TO HAMPSTEAD.

[" Examiner," Dec. 18th, 1814. "Feast of the Poets,"
2nd ed., 1815. "Works," 1860.]

WINTER has reached thee once again at
  last ;
  And now the rambler, whom thy
   groves yet please,
 Feels on his house-warm lips the thin air freeze,
While in his shrugging neck the resolute blast
Comes edging ; and the leaves, in heaps down
  cast,
 He shuffles with his hastening foot, and sees
 The cold sky whitening through the wiry trees,
And sighs to think his loitering noons have passed.

And do I love thee less to paint thee so ?
 No : this the season is of beauty still,
  Doubled at heart ; of smoke, with whirling
   glee
Uptumbling ever from the blaze below,
 And home remembered most,—and oh, loved
  hill,
  The second, and the last, away from thee.·

SURREY JAIL, *Nov.*, 1814.

VI.

TO HAMPSTEAD.

[" Examiner," May 7th, 1815. " Feast of the Poets,"
2nd ed., 1815. " Works," 1860.]

HE baffled spell that bound me is un-
    done,
    And I have breathed once more
      beneath thy sky,
Lovely-browed Hampstead ; and my looks have
    run,
  O'er and about thee, and had scarce drawn
    nigh,
When I beheld, in momentary sun,
  One of thy hills gleam bright and bosomy,
Just like that orb of orbs, a human one,
  Let forth by chance upon a lover's eye.

Forgive me then, that not before I spoke ;
  Since all the comforts, miss'd in close distress,
    With airy nod came up from every part,
O'er-smiling speech : and so I gazed and took
  A long, deep draught of silent freshfulness,
    Ample, and gushing round my fevered heart.

May 3rd, 1815.

VII.

TO HAMPSTEAD.

["Examiner," May 7th, 1815. "Feast of the Poets,"
2nd ed., 1815. "Works," 1860. "Canterbury Poets,"
1889.]

S one who after long and far-spent
    years
    Comes on his mistress in an hour of
    sleep,
And half surprised that he can silence keep,
Stands smiling o'er her through a flash of tears,
To see how sweet and self-same she appears;
    Till at his touch, with little moving creep
    Of joy, she wakes from out her calmness deep,
And then his heart finds voice, and dances round
    her ears:—

So I, first coming on my haunts again,
    In pause and stillness of the early prime,
    Stood thinking of the past and present time
With earnest eyesight, scarcely crossed with pain;
    Till the fresh-moving leaves, and startling birds,
    Loosened my long-suspended breath in words.

VII.

TO HAMPSTEAD.

["Examiner," Nov. 12th, 1815. "Foliage," 1818.
"Rimini," &c., 1844.]

STEEPLE issuing from a leafy rise,
With farmy fields in front, and sloping
green,
Dear Hampstead, is thy southern face
serene,
Silently smiling on approaching eyes,
Within, thine ever-shifting looks surprise,
Streets, hills, and dells, trees overhead now seen,
Now down below, with smoking roofs between,—
A village, revelling in varieties.
Then northward what a range,—with heath and
pond,
Nature's own ground; woods that let mansions
through,
And cottaged vales with pillowy fields beyond,
And clump of darkening pines, and prospects blue,
And that clear path through all, where daily meet
Cool cheeks, and brilliant eyes, and morn-elastic
feet.

TO KOSCIUSKO.[1]

Who took part neither with Bonaparte in the height of his
power, nor with the allies in the height of theirs.

["Examiner," Nov. 19th, 1815. "Foliage," 1818.
"Living Poets of England" (Paris), 1827. "Works,"
1832, 1844, 1857, 1860. "Book of Sonnets," 1867. "Canterbury Poets," 1889.]

'TIS like thy patient valour thus to keep,
  Great Kosciusko, to the rural shade,
  While Freedom's ill-found amulet
   still is made
Pretence for old aggression, and a heap
Of selfish mockeries.   There, as in the sweep
  Of stormier fields, thou earnest with thy blade,
  Transformed, not inly altered, to the spade,
Thy never yielding right to a calm sleep.

Nature, 'twould seem, would leave to man's worse
    wit,
The small and noisier part of this world's frame,
And keep the calm, green amplitudes of it
Sacred from fopperies and inconstant blame.
Cities may change, and sovereigns, but 'tis fit,
Thou and the country old be still the same !

[1] In the 1832 and later editions the second verse was
printed thus :—

  "There came a wanderer, borne from land to land
   Upon a couch, pale, many-wounded, mild,
    His brow with patient pain dulcetly sour.
  Men stoop'd with awful sweetness on his hand,
   And kiss'd it ; and collected Virtue smiled,
    To think how sovereign her enduring hour."

THE POETS.

[The " Examiner," Dec. 24th, 1815.]

ERE I to name, out of the times
    gone by,
    The poets dearest to me, I should
    say,
Pulci for spirits, and a fine free way ;
Chaucer for manners, and close, silent eye ;
Milton for classic taste, and harp strung high ;
    Spenser for luxury, and sweet, sylvan play ;
    Horace for chatting with from day to day ;
Shakespeare for all, but most society.

But which take with me, could I take but one?
    Shakespeare—as long as I was unoppressed
With the world's weight, making sad thoughts
    intenser ;
But did I wish, out of the common sun,
    To lay a wounded heart in leafy rest,
And dream of things far off and healing—Spenser.

PROVIDENCE.

FROM THE ITALIAN OF FILICIA.

[" Examiner," March 10th, 1816.]

UST as a mother with sweet pious face
    Yearns towards her little children
    from her seat,
    Gives one a kiss, another an embrace,
Takes this upon her knee, that on her feet ;

And while from actions, looks, complaints, pre-
   tences
  She learns their feelings and their various will,
To this a look, to that a word dispenses,
  And whether stern or smiling, loves them still :

So Providence for us, high, infinite,
Makes our necessities its watchful task,
Hearkens to all our prayers, helps all our wants ;
And even if it denies what seems our right,
Either denies because 'twould have us ask,
Or seems but to deny, or in denying grants.

ON A LOCK OF MILTON'S HAIR.[1]

["Foliage," 1818. "Works," 1832, 1844, 1857, 1860.
"Book of Sonnets," 1867. "Favourite Poems," 1877.
Kent, 1889. "Canterbury Poets," 1889.]

IT lies before me there, and my own
     breath
     Stirs its thin outer threads, as though
     beside
The living head I stood in honoured pride,
Talking of lovely things that conquer death.
Perhaps he pressed it once, or underneath
  Ran his fine fingers, when he leant, blank-eyed,
  And saw, in fancy, Adam and his bride
With their rich locks, or his own Delphic wreath.

[1] Leigh Hunt refers to this particular lock, and to his
collection of the hair of great men, in one of the "New
Wishing-Cap Papers," in "Tait's Magazine," 1833. Keats
also wrote a few verses on this subject, perhaps inspired by
the same lock, for he speaks of only seeing one, not possessing it.—ED.

There seems a love in hair, though it be dead.
It is the gentlest, yet the strongest thread
  Of our frail plant,—a blossom from the tree
Surviving the proud trunk :—as though it said
  Patience and Gentleness is Power.   In me
Behold affectionate eternity.

THE NILE.[1]

["Foliage," 1818. " Living Poets of England" (Paris),
1827. "Works," 1832, 1857, 1860. "Book of Sonnets,"
1867. "Rimini," &c., 1844. "Canterbury Poets," 1889.
"Macmillan's Magazine," 1889.]

T flows through old hushed Ægypt and
      its sands,
         Like some grave mighty thought
            threading a dream,
  And times and things, as in that vision, seem
Keeping along it their eternal stands,—
Caves, pillars, pyramids, the shepherd bands
  That roamed through the young world, the glory
      extreme
Of high Sesostris, and that southern beam,
The laughing queen that caught the world's great
      hands.

Then comes a mightier silence, stern and strong,
As of a world left empty of its throng,

---

1 " The Wednesday before last, Shelley, Hunt, and I,
wrote each a sonnet on the river Nile ; some day you shall
read them all." Letter of John Keats, February, 1818.
All three sonnets are printed in the Aldine Edition of Keats'
Works.—ED.

And the void weighs on us ; and then we
    wake,
And hear the fruitful stream lapsing along
  'Twixt villages, and think how we shall take
  Our own calm journey on for human sake.[1]

CALVIULTOR.

Written in the character of a bald man in answer to a clever
sonnet against baldness.

[Copied from MS. in the Forster Library, South Kensington Museum.]

'VE got my wig :—and now, thou rash
      Hirsutus,
  Crinitus, Whiskerandos, Ogre, Bear,
  Or whatsoever title please thine hair,
Why vex the bald ? Why loveless thus repute us ?
Great Shakespeare, *omni nectare imbutus*,
Was bald ; and he, whose age knew no despair,
Socrates, dancer 'midst the young and fair,
And Cæsar, victim of a *natural* Brutus !

Fresh is the bald man's head ; for love so apt,
That England's Gallants, in her wittiest time,
In voluntary baldness, velvet capp'd,
Through reams of letters urged their amorous
    rhyme :

[1] The eighth line of the above sonnet, as Mr. Saintsbury
points out, is a rediscovery of a cadence which had been lost
for centuries, and which has been constantly borrowed and
imitated since.

Then issued forth, peruked, and o'er their
    shoulders
From every curl shook love at all the fair be-
    holders.

ARIOSTO'S PRISON.[1]

["Indicator," No. XX., Feb. 23rd, 1820. "Works,"
1832.]

LUCKY prison, blithe captivity,
    Where neither out of rage nor out of
        spite,
    But bound by love and charity's sweet
        might,
She has me fast—my lovely enemy ;
Others, at turning of their prison key,
Sadden ; I triumph ; since I have in sight
Not death but life, not suffering but delight,
Nor law severe, nor judge that hears no plea ;

But gatherings to the heart, but wilful blisses,
But words that in such moments are no crimes,
But laughs and tricks and winning ways ; but
    kisses,
Delicious kisses put deliciously,
A thousand, thousand, thousand, thousand times
And yet how few will all those thousands be.

[1] Called "The Lover's Prison" in 1832 ed.—ED.

A HEAVEN UPON EARTH.

Fragment of an unpublished play. A husband is
conversing with his wife.

["Works," 1844, 1857, 1860. Kent, 1889.]

FOR there are two heavens, sweet,
  Both made of love,—one, inconceiv-
    able
  Ev'n by the other, so divine it is ;
The other, far on *this* side of the stars,
By men called *home*, when some blest pair are met
As we are now ; sometimes in happy talk,
Sometimes in silence (also a sort of talk,
Where friends are matched) each at its gentle task
Of book, or household need, or meditation,
By summer-moon, or curtained fire in frost ;
And by degrees there come,—not always come,
Yet mostly,—other, smaller inmates there,
Cherubic-faced, yet growing like those two,
Their pride and playmates, not without meek fear,
Since God sometimes to his own cherubim
Takes those sweet cheeks of earth.   And so 'twixt
   joy,
And love, and tears, and whatsoever pain
Man fitly shares with man, these two grow old ; ·
And if indeed blest thoroughly, they die
In the same spot, and nigh the same good hour,
And setting suns look heavenly on their grave.—

PAGANINI.

["London Journal," April 16th, 1834, from an unpublished poem by the editor. "Works," 1844, 1857, 1860. Kent, 1889.]

O played of late to every passing thought
With finest change (might I but half as
    well
So write!) the pale magician of the
    bow,
Who brought from Italy the tales, made true,
Of Grecian lyres; and on his sphery hand,
Loading the air with dumb expectancy,
Suspended, ere it fell, a nation's breath.

He smote—and clinging to the serious chords
With godlike ravishment, drew forth a breath,
So deep, so strong, so fervid thick with love,
Blissful, yet laden as with twenty prayers,
That Juno yearned with no diviner soul
To the first burthen of the lips of Jove.

The exceeding mystery of the loveliness
Saddened delight; and with his mournful look,
Dreary and gaunt, hanging his pallid face
'Twixt his dark flowing locks, he almost seemed,
To feeble or to melancholy eyes,
One that had parted with his soul for pride,
And in the sable secret lived forlorn.

But true and earnest, all too happily
That skill dwelt in him, serious with its joy;
For noble now he smote the exulting strings,

And bade them march before his stately will ;
And now he loved them like a cheek, and laid
Endearment on them, and took pity sweet ;
And now he was all mirth, or all for sense
And reason, carving out his thoughts like prose
After his poetry ; or else he laid
His own soul prostrate at the feet of love,
And with a full and trembling fervour deep,
In kneeling and close-creeping urgency,
Implored some mistress with hot tears ; which
      past,
And after patience had brought right of peace,
He drew, as if from thoughts finer than hope,
Comfort around him in ear-soothing strains
And elegant composure ; or he turned
To heaven instead of earth, and raised a pray'r
So earnest vehement, yet so lowly sad,
Mighty with want and all poor human tears,
That never saint, wrestling with earthly love
And in mid-age unable to get free,
Tore down from heav'n such pity. Or behold,
In his despair (for such, from what he spoke
Of grief before it, or of love, 'twould seem),
Jump would he into some strange wail uncouth
Of witches' dance, ghastly with whinings thin
And palsied nods—mirth wicked, sad, and weak,
And then with show of skill mechanical,
Marvellous as witchcraft, he would overthrow
That vision with a show'r of notes like hail,
Or sudden mixtures of all difficult things
Never yet heard ; flashing the sharp tones now,
In downward leaps like swords ; now rising fine
Into some utmost tip of minute sound,

From whence he stepped into a higher and higher
On viewless points, till laugh took leave of him :
Or he would fly as if from all the world
To be alone, and happy, and you should hear
His instrument become a tree far off,
A nest of birds and sunbeams, sparkling both,
A cottage bow'r : or he would condescend,
In playful wisdom which knows no contempt,
To bring to laughing memory, plain as sight,
A farmyard with its inmates, ox and lamb,
The whistle and the whip, with feeding hens
In household fidget muttering evermore,
And, rising as in scorn, crowned Chanticleer,
Ordaining silence with his sovereign crow.
Then from one chord of his amazing shell
Would he fetch out the voice of quires, and weight
Of the built organ ; or some twofold strain
Moving before him in sweet-going yoke,
Ride like an Eastern conqueror, round whose state
Some light Morisco leaps with his guitar ;
And ever and anon o'er these he'd throw
Jets of small notes like pearl, or like the pelt
Of lovers' sweetmeats on Italian lutes
From windows on a feast-day, or the leaps
Of pebbled water, sprinkling in the sun,
One chord effecting all :—and when the ear
Felt there was nothing present but himself
And silence, and the wonder drew deep sighs,
Then would his bow lie down again in tears,
And speak to some one in a pray'r of love,
Endless, and never from his heart to go :
Or he would talk as of some secret bliss,
And at the close of all the wonderment

II.   H

(Which himself shared) near and more near would
    come
Into the inmost ear, and whisper there
Breathings so soft, so low, so full of life,
Touched beyond sense, and only to be borne
By pauses which made each less bearable,
That out of pure necessity for relief
From that heaped joy, and bliss that laughed for
    pain,
The thunder of th' uprolling house came down,
And bowed the breathing sorcerer into smiles.

THE MAD GIRL'S SONG.

SEPT. 11, 1800.

[" Juvenilia," 1801.]

THE lily enamels the vale,
    The roses they purple above ;
But how can their glories prevail
    With a smile from the lips of my
    Love ?
But my Love, he was false and unkind,
    When he bade me depart from the grove :
And I'll go : for I have not a mind
    That will laugh in the frowns of my Love.

I'll pick up the flow'rs that are dead,
    And deck all my bosom so gay,
And Love shall come patting my head,
    And steal all their blossoms away.

But, no ; he shan't rob me of these,
   Refusal his wishes shall prove :
For he would not, my passions to please,
   Inspire the cold breast of my Love.

I will visit the cypress so sad,
   That hangs o'er the dark-shadowed grave ;
And I know, tho' they tell me I'm mad,
   That I'll tear off its branches to wave.
O, and then a sweet garland I'll twine,
   And shew all my friends how I wove ;
And all but the leaves shall be mine,
   For I'll give all the green to my Love.

But my Love, I'm afraid, won't be pressed
   To take the poor gift, tho' so smart :
For he scorned this poor fluttering breast,
   And all the warm wealth of my heart.
Then I'll keep it and twine in my hair
   The green, and the boughs that I wove ;
And when it shall fade away there,
   Sing dirges to it and my Love.

MORGIANA IN ENGLAND.

AIR—*The De'il came fiddling through the town.*

1815.

["Feast of the Poets," 2nd ed., 1815. "Works," 1857, 1860.]

OH, one that I know is a knavish lass,
　　Though she looks so sweet and simple ;
　Her eyes there are none can safely pass,
　　And it's wrong to trust her dimple.
So taking the jade was by Nature made,
　So finished in all fine thieving,
She'll e'en look away what you wanted to say,
　And smile you out of your grieving.

To see her, for instance, go down a dance,
　You'd think you sat securely,
There's nothing about her of forward France,
　And nothing done over demurely :
But Lord ! she goes with so blithe a repose,
　And comes so shapely about you,
That ere you're aware, with a glance and an air
　She whisks your heart from out you.

SONG.

MYRTILLA TO UNKNOWN SPIRIT.

[" Descent of Liberty," 1815.]

ENTLE and unknown delight,
    Hovering with thy music near us,
If that our request be right,
    Lean thou tow'rd the earth, and hear
        us;
And if we may yet rejoice,
Touch the silence with a voice.

By the lingering day forlorn,
    And the dread of drear to-morrow,
By the infant yet unborn,
    Waiting for its world of sorrow,
By youth, forgetful to rejoice,
And middle age's failing voice;

By the griefs of many lands,
    And hearts that waste in secret places,
By the lift of trembling hands,
    And the tears on furrowed faces,
Say, shall anguish yet rejoice?
Spirit dear, put forth a voice.

SONG.

DIFFERENT GENII TO PEACE.

[" Descent of Liberty," 1815.]

WRAPPING looks and balmy tongue,
  Sweet as summer air through tree,
Remembered when this age was young,
  Like sights beheld in infancy,
O Peace, whose very name's a pleasure,
    Reappear,
    To bless us here,
And light with silken foot upon our leisure !

By the last tear that hangs to-day,
For thy kiss to clip away ;
By the toil of struggling hearts,
That rest them from their final parts ;
By hopes that wait in rising lands,
A blessing from thy gentle hands ;

By home delights, and spirits free,
And one full sigh of earth and sea,
And victorious Liberty ;
    Reappear, reappear !
Earth is worthy to regain thee,
And hopes it may not always pain thee.

EPILOGUE TO THE DESCENT OF LIBERTY. 1815.

POETA LOQUITUR.

'TIS done.   The vision from my fancy's
           eye
     Fades, gleam by gleam, into the closing
           sky ;
And the far sounds, touching from sphere to sphere
With upward lessening, baffle the fixed ear,
But not directly does the earthly chain,
That holds me here, come closing round again ;
Not instantly the darkening wall comes nigh ;
The brightened spot yet breathes of Liberty ;
The fine and holier circle charms me still,
Drawn by the quickness of the Muse's quill ;
And silence, listening as at dead of night,
Sits with her finger up, hushing Delight.

TO WILLIAM HAZLITT.

["Examiner," July 14th, 1816.   "Foliage," 1818.
"Works," 1857, 1860.]

Et modo qua nostri spatiantur in urbe quirites,
Et modo villarum proxima rura placent.— MILTON, *Eleg.* 7.
Enjoying now the range of town at ease,
And now the neighbouring rural villages.

DEAR H[AZLITT] whose tact intellec-
           tual is such,   .
     That it seems to feel truth, as one's
           fingers do touch,—
Who in politics, arts, metaphysics, poetics,

To critics in these times, art health to cosmetics,
And, nevertheless, or I rather should say,
For that very reason,—can relish boy's play,
And turning on all sides, through pleasures and
        cares,
Find nothing more precious than laughs and fresh
        airs,—

One's life, I conceive, might go prettily down,
In a due easy mixture of country and town ;—
Not after the fashion of most with two houses,
Who gossip, and gape, and just follow their spouses,
And let their abode be wherever it will,
Are the same vacant, house-keeping animals
        still ;—
But with due sense of each, and of all that it
        yields,—
In the town, of the town,—in the fields, of the
        fields ;
In the one, for example, to feel as we go on,
That streets are about us, arts, people, and so
        on ;
In t'other, to value the stillness, the breeze,
And love to see farms, and to get among trees.

Each his liking, of course,—so that this be the
        rule.—
For my part, who went in the city to school,
And whenever I got in a field, felt my soul in it
—*Spring*, so that like a young horse I could roll
        in it,—
—*My* inclinations are much what they were,
And cannot dispense, in the first place, with air ;

But then I would have the most rural of nooks
Just near enough town to make use of its books,
And to walk there, whenever I chose to make calls,
To look at the ladies, and lounge at the stalls.

To tell you the truth, I could spend very well
Whole mornings in this way 'twixt here and Pall
    Mall,
And make my gloves' fingers as black as my hat,
In pulling the books up from this stall and that :—
Then turning home gently through field and o'er
    style,
Partly reading a purchase, or rhyming the while,
Take my dinner (to make a long evening) at two,
With a few droppers-in, like my Cousin and you,
Who can season the talk with the right-flavoured
    Attic,
Too witty, for tattling,—too wise, for dogmatic ;—
Then take down an author, whom one of us men-
    tions,
And doat, for a while, on his jokes or inventions ;
Then have Mozart touched on our bottle's com-
    pletion,
Or one of your fav'rite trim ballads Venetian :—
Then up for a walk before tea down a valley,
And so to come back through a leafy-wall'd alley,
In which the sun peeping, as into a chamber,
Looks gold on the leaves, turning some to sheer
    amber :
Then tea made by one, who (although my wife
    she be,)
If Jove were to drink it, would soon be his Hebe ;
Then silence a little,—a creeping twilight,—

Then an egg for your supper, with lettuces white,
And a moon and friend's arm to go home with at
    night.

Now this I call passing a few devout hours
Becoming a world that has friendships and flowers ;
That has lips also, made for still more than to
    chat to ;
And if it has rain, has a rainbow for that too.
"Lord bless us !" exclaims some old hunks in a
    shop,
"What useless young dogs !" and falls combing a
    crop.
"How idle !" another cries—"really a sin !"
And starting up, takes his first customer in.
"At least," cries another, "it's nothing but plea-
    sure ; "
Then longs for the Monday, quite sick of his
    leisure.
"What toys !" cries the sage haggard statesman,
    —"what stuff ! "
Then fillips his riband, to shake off the snuff.
"How profane !" cries the preacher, proclaiming
    his message ;
Then calls God's creation a vile dirty passage.
"Lips too !" cries a vixen,—and fidgets, and stirs,
And concludes (which is true) that I didn't mean
    hers.

Yet most of these sages, dear Will, would agree,
To get what they could out of you and of me,—
To stir up their jog-trotting dullness at times
With your cannonade reas'ning, or dance of my
    rhymes.

They only would have us dig on like themselves,
Yet bè all observation to furnish their shelves ;
Would only expect us (inordinate crew !)
To be just what they are, and delight them all too !
As well might they ask the explorers of oceans
To make their discoveries, as doctors do lotions ;
Or shut up some bees in the till with the money,
And look, on the Sabbath, to breakfast on honey.

The secret, in fact, why most people condemn,
Is not that men differ, but differ with them.
And yet if the world were put under their keeping,
Our only resource from a pond would be sleeping.
I've thought of, sometimes when amused with these
    cavils,
A passage I met with in somebody's travels, —
A merchant's, —who sailing from Greece to Triësté,
Grew vexed with the crew, and avowedly testy,
Because, as he said, being lazy and Greeks,
They were always for putting in harbours and
    creeks,
And instead of conveying him quick with his lading,
(As any men would, who had due sense of trading)
Could never come near a green isle with a spring,
But smack they went to it, like birds on the wing ;
And taking their wine out, and strumming their
    lutes,
Fell drinking and dancing,—like so many brutes.

Ah, Will, there are some birds and beasts, I'm
    afraid,
Who if they could peep upon some of the trade,
And see them pale, sneaking, proud, faithless of
    trust,

Midst their wainscotted twilight, and bundles, and
    dust,
Would wonder what strange kind of nest and of
    blisses
The creatures had picked up from a world such as
    this is.
Imagine, for instance, a lark at the casement
Stand glancing his head about, deep in amazement;
Then turning it up to the cloud-silvered skies,
Strikes off to the fields with the air in his eyes,
And heaving and heaving,—thrilled, quivering,
    and even,
Goes mounting his steps of wild music to heaven.

    I blame (you'll bear witness) these tricksters and
    hiders
No more than I quarrel with bats or with spiders—
All, all have their uses, though never so hideous—
But bats shouldn't fancy their eyesight prodigious.

    You see I can't mention the country again,
But I'm off like a Harlequin, plump through the
    pane.
I forget I'm in town and have letters to write
To my cousin [1] about it, and so, sir, Good-night.
P.S. No news of the Bourbons.   You've heard
    of the blight?

[1] This and the following poem are described as letters
from Harry Brown to his friends, those to Thomas Moore
are superscribed " to his cousin, Thomas Brown."—ED.

TO CHARLES LAMB.

["Examiner," Aug. 25th, 1816. "Foliage," 1818.
"Works," 1857, 1860.]

THOU, whom old Homer would call,
    were he living,
    Home-lover, thought-feeder, abundant-
    joke-giving;
Whose charity springs from deep knowledge, nor
    swerves
Into mere self-reflections, or scornful reserves;
In short, who were made for two centuries ago,
When Shakespeare drew men, and to write was to
    know ;—

You'll not be surprised that I can't walk the
    streets,
Without thinking of you and your visiting feats,
When you call to remembrance how you and one
    more,
When I wanted it most, used to knock at my door.
For when the sad winds told us rain would come
    down,
Or snow upon snow fairly clogged up the town,
And dun yellow fogs brooded over its white,
So that scarcely a being was seen towards night,
Then, then said the lady yclept near and dear,
" Now mind what I tell you, the L[amb]s will be
    here."
So I poked up the flame, and she got out the tea,
And down we both sat, as prepared as could be;

And there, sure as fate, came the knock of you two.
Then the lantern, the laugh, and the " Well, how
    d'ye do ? "
Then your palm tow'rds the fire, and your face
    turned to me,
And shawls and great-coats being—where they
    should be,—
And due " never saw's " being paid to the weather,
We cherished our knees, and sat sipping together,
And leaving the world to the fogs and the fighters,
Discussed the pretensions of all sorts of writers ;
Of Shakespeare's coëvals, all spirits divine ;
Of Chapman, whose Homer's a fine rough old wine ;
Of Marvell, wit, patriot, and poet, who knew
How to give, both at once, Charles and Cromwell
    their due.
Of Spenser, who wraps you, wherever you are,
In a bow'r of seclusion beneath a sweet star ;
Of Richardson, too, who afflicts us so long,
We begin to suspect him of nerves over strong ;
In short, of all those who give full-measured
    page,
Not forgetting Sir Thomas,[1] my ancestor sage,
Who delighted (so happy were all his digestions)
In puzzling his head with impossible questions.

But *now*, Charles—you never (so blissful you
    deem me)
Come lounging, with twirl of umbrella to see me.
In vain have we hoped to be set at our ease
By the rains which you know used to bring Lamb
    and pease ;

[1] *i.e.* Sir Thomas Browne.

In vain we look out like the children in Thomson,
And say, in our innocence, " Surely, he'll come
　　soon."

　'Tis true, I do live in a vale, at my will,
With sward to my gateway, and trees on the hill :
My health too gets on : and now autumn is nigh,
The sun has come back, and there's really blue
　　sky ;
But then, the late weather, I think, had its merits,
And might have induced you to look at one's
　　spirits ;
We hadn't much thunder and lightning, I own :
But the rains might have led you to walk out of
　　town ;
And what made us think your desertion still
　　stranger,
The roads were so bad, there was really some
　　danger ;
At least where I live ; for the nights were so
　　groping,
The rains made such wet, and the paths were so
　　sloping,
That few, unemboldened by youth or by drinking,
Came down without lanthorns,—nor then without
　　shrinking.
And really, to see the bright spots come and go,
As the path rose or fell, was a fanciful shew.
Like fairies they seemed, pitching up from their
　　nooks,
And twinkling upon us their bright little looks ;
Or if there appeared but a single slow light,
It seemed Polyphemus, descending by night

To walk in his anguish about the green places,
To see where his mistress lie dreaming of Acis.

I fancy him now, coming just where she sleeps ;
He parts the close hawthorns, and bushes, and
     creeps ;—
The moon slips from under the dark clouds, and
     throws
A light, through the leaves, on her smiling repose,
There, there she lies, bowered ;—a slope for her
     bed ;
One branch, like a hand, reaches over her head ;
Half naked, half shrinking, with side-swelling
     grace,
A crook's 'twixt her bosom, and crosses her face,—
The crook of her shepherd ;—and close to her lips
Lies the Pan-pipe he blows, which in sleeping she
     sips ;—
The giant's knees totter, with passions diverse ;
Ah, how can he bear it ! ah, what could be worse !
He's ready to cry out, for anguish of heart ;
And tears himself off, lest she wake with a start.
So much for the *streets* I gave out as my text,
But of these my dear L[amb] you must hear in my
     next.

TO T. L. H.[1]

SIX YEARS OLD, DURING A SICKNESS.

[" Examiner," Sept. 1st, 1816. " Foliage," 1818. " Living Poets of England " (Paris), 1827. " Works," 1832, 1844, 1857, 1860. " Rimini," &c., 1844. Kent, 1889. " Canterbury Poets," 1889.]

LEEP breathes at last from out thee,
　My little, patient boy ;
And balmy rest about thee
　Smooths off the day's annoy.
　　I sit me down, and think
　　Of all thy winning ways ;
Yet almost wish, with sudden shrink,
　　That I had less to praise.

Thy sidelong pillowed meekness,
　Thy thanks to all that aid,
Thy heart, in pain and weakness,
　Of fancied faults afraid ;
　　The little trembling hand
　　That wipes thy quiet tears,
These, these are things that may demand
　　Dread memories for years.

Sorrows I've had, severe ones,
　I will not think of now ;
And calmly 'midst my dear ones
　Have wasted with dry brow ;
　　But when thy fingers press
　　And pat my stooping head,

[1] A child who had also the honour of being addressed in verse by Charles Lamb, in some lines which appeared in the " Examiner," 1815.—ED.

I cannot bear the gentleness,—
    The tears are in their bed.

Ah, first-born of thy mother,
    When life and hope were new,
Kind playmate of thy brother,
    Thy sister, father too ;
        My light, where'er I go,
        My bird, when prison-bound,
My hand in hand companion,—no,
        My prayers shall hold thee round.

To say " He has departed "—
    " His voice "—" his face "—is gone ;
To feel impatient-hearted,
    Yet feel we must bear on ;
        Ah, I could not endure
        To whisper of such woe,
Unless I felt this sleep ensure
        That it will not be so.

Yes, still he's fixed, and sleeping !
    This silence too the while—
Its very hush and creeping
    Seem whispering us a smile :
        Something divine and dim
        Seems going by one's ear,
Like parting wings of Seraphim,
        Who say, " We've finished here."

ARIADNE WAKING.

["Bacchus and Ariadne," 1819.   "Works," 1832.
" Rimini, and other poems," Boston, 1844.]

THE moist and quiet moon was scarcely
              breaking,
When Ariadne in her bower was
              waking ;
Her eyelids still were closing, and she heard
But indistinctly yet a little bird,
That in the leaves o'erhead, waiting the sun,
Seemed answering another distant one.
She waked but stirred not, only just to please
Her pillow-nestling cheek ; while the full seas,
The birds, the leaves, the lulling love o'ernight,
The happy thought of the returning light,
The sweet, self-willed content, conspired to keep
Her senses lingering in the feel of sleep ;
And with a little smile she seemed to say,
" I know my love is near me, and 'tis day."

SONG

FROM THE ITALIAN BEGINNING

Arancie, bella arancie ;
Pienotte come guencie ;

[" Indicator," July 5th, 1820. " Romancist and Novelist's Library," edited by W. Hazlitt, 1839.]

H oranges, sweet oranges,
  Plumpy cheeks that peep in trees,
  The crabbed'st churl in all the south
  Would hardly let a thirsty mouth
Gaze at ye, and long to taste,
Nor grant one golden kiss at last.
  La, la, la,—la sol fa mi—
  My Lady looked through the orange tree.

Yet cheeks there are, yet cheeks there are,
Sweeter—oh good God ; how far !—
That make a thirst like very death
Down to the heart through lips and breath,
And if we asked a taste of those,
The kindest owners would turn foes,
  O la, la,—la sol fa mi—
  My Lady's gone from the orange tree.

CHORUS.

[From "Amyntas," 1820.]

HERE is no need of death
To bind a great heart fast ;
Faith is enough at first, and Love at
last.
Nor does a fond desert
Pursue so hard a fame
In following its sweet aim ;
Since Love is paid with its own loving heart,
And oftentimes, ere it work out its story,
It finds itself clasp glory.

THE NUN.

SUGGESTED BY FIRST FOUR LINES OF THE VENETIAN AIR BEGINNING,

" Se moneca ti fai."

["Indicator," No. LXV., Jan. 3rd, 1821. "Works," 1832.]

IF you become a nun, dear,
A friar I will be ;
In any cell you run, dear,
Pray look behind for me.
The rose, of course, turns pale too ;
The doves all take the veil too ;
The blind will see the show ;
What ! you become a nun, my dear ?
I'll not believe it, no.

If you become a nun, dear,
　　The bishop Love will be ;
The cupids every one, dear,
　　Will chaunt " we trust in thee : "
The incense will go sighing,
The candles fall a dying,
　　The water turn to wine :
What ! you go take the vows, my dear ?
　　You may—but they'll be mine.

SUDDEN FINE WEATHER.[1]

[" Tatler," July 30th, 1831. "Works," 1832, 1844, 1857,
1860. "Rimini," &c., 1844. Kent, 1889.]

READER ! what soul that loves a verse,
　　　　can see
　　　　The spring return, nor glow like you
　　　　and me?
Hear the rich birds, and see the landscape fill,
Nor long to utter his harmonious [2] will ?

　This more than ever leaps into the veins,
When spring has been delayed by winds and rains,
And coming with a burst, comes like a show,
Blue all above, and basking green below,

---

1 In the 1832 edition this is called "Lines written in May."
In the "Tatler" the poem is described as being extracted
from the forthcoming number of the " Englishman's Magazine."—ED.

2 In most editions this word is "melodious," but in the
" Autobiography," vol. iii., p. 197, where the whole poem is
discussed, L. H. says that it should be "harmonious."—ED.

And all the people culling the sweet prime : ⎫
Then issues forth the bee to clutch the thyme, ⎬
And the bee poet rushes into rhyme. ⎭

    For lo ! no sooner have the chills withdrawn,
Than the bright elm is tufted on the lawn ;
The merry sap has run up in the bowers,
And bursts the windows of the buds in flowers ; ·
With song the bosoms of the birds run o'er,
The cuckoo calls, the swallow's at the door,
And apple-trees at noon, with bees alive,
Burn with the golden chorus of the hive.
Now all these sweets, these sounds, this vernal
      blaze,
Is but one joy, expressed a thousand ways :
And honey from the flowers, and song from
      birds,
Are from the poet's pen his overflowing words.

    Ah friends ! methinks it were a pleasant sphere,
If, like the trees, we blossom'd every year ;
If locks grew thick again, and rosy dyes
Returned in cheeks, and raciness in eyes,
And all around us, vital to the tips,
The human orchard laughed with cherry lips !

    Lord ! what a burst of merriment and play,
Fair dames, were that ! and what a first of May !

    So natural is the wish, that bards gone by
Have left it, all, in some immortal sigh !

    And yet the winter months were not so well :
Who would like changing, as the seasons fell ?

Fade every year ; and stare, midst ghastly friends,
With falling hairs, and stuck-out fingers' ends ?
Besides, this tale of youth that comes again,
Is no more true of apple-trees than men.
The Swedish sage, the Newton of the flow'rs,
Who first found out those worlds of paramours,
Tells us, that every blossom that we see
Boasts in its walls a separate family ;
So that a tree is but a sort of stand,
That holds those filial fairies in its hand ;
Just as Swift's giant might have held a bevy
Of Lilliputian ladies, or a levee.
It is not he that blooms : it is his race,
Who honour his old arms, and hide his rugged
      face.

   Ye wits and bards then, pray discern your duty,
And learn the *lastingness* of human beauty.
Your finest fruit to some two months may reach :
I've known a cheek at *forty* like a peach.

   But see ! the weather calls me.   Here's a bee
Comes bounding in my room imperiously,
And talking to himself, hastily burns
About mine ear, and so in heat returns.
O little brethren of the fervid soul,
Kissers of flowers, lords of the golden bowl,
I follow to your fields and tufted brooks :
Winter's the time to which the poet looks
For hiving his sweet thoughts, and making honied
      books.

SONGS AND CHORUS OF FLOWERS.

["New Monthly Magazine," May, 1836. "Works,"
1844, 1857, 1860. "Favourite Poems," 1877.]

ROSES.[1]

WE are blushing Roses,
    Bending with our fulness,
'Midst our close-capped sister buds,
    Warming the green coolness.

Whatsoe'er of beauty
    Yearns and yet reposes,
Blush, and bosom, and sweet breath,
    Took a shape in roses.

Hold one of us lightly,—
    See from what a slender
Stalk we bow'r in heavy blooms,
    And roundness rich and tender.

Know you not our only
    Rival flow'r—the human?
Loveliest weight on lightest foot,
    Joy-abundant woman?

POPPIES.

We are slumberous poppies,
    Lords of Lethe downs,
Some awake, and some asleep,
    Sleeping in our crowns.

[1] See also translation from Anacreon with this title, given below.—ED.

What perchance our dreams may know,
Let our serious beauty show.

Central depth of purple,
　Leaves more bright than rose,
Who shall tell what brightest thought
　Out of darkest grows ?
Who, through what funereal pain
Souls to love and peace attain ?

Visions aye are on us,
　Unto eyes of power,
Pluto's always setting sun,
　And Proserpine's bower :
There, like bees, the pale souls come
For our drink with drowsy hum.

Taste, ye mortals, also ;
　Milky-hearted, we ;
Taste, but with a reverent care ;
　Active-patient be.
Too much gladness brings to gloom
Those who on the gods presume.[1]

[1] Opium is chiefly made from the white poppy, but the red is the one so much better known, that the writer has here made it stand for the whole genus.

CHORUS OF THE FLOWERS.

[This part has also been reprinted in Kent, 1889, and " Canterbury Poets," 1890.]

W E are the sweet Flowers,
   Born of sunny showers,
  (Think, whene'er you see us, what our
    beauty saith :)
  Utterance mute and bright
  Of some unknown delight,
We fill the air with pleasure, by our simple breath :
   All who see us, love us ;
   We befit all places ;
Unto sorrow we give smiles ; and unto graces,
   graces.

   Mark our ways, how noiseless
   All, and sweetly voiceless,
Though the March winds pipe to make our passage
   clear ;
   Not a whisper tells
   Where our small seed dwells,
Nor is known the moment green, when our tips
   appear.
   We thread the earth in silence,
   In silence build our bowers,
And leaf by leaf in silence shew, till we laugh atop,
   sweet Flowers !

   The dear lumpish baby,
   Humming with the May-bee,

Hails us with his bright stare, stumbling through
    the grass ;
    The honey-dropping moon,
    On a night in June,
Kisses our pale pathway leaves, that felt the bride-
    groom pass.
    Age, the withered clinger,
    On us mutely gazes,
And wraps the thought of his last bed in his child-
    hood's daisies.

    See (and scorn all duller
    Taste), how heav'n loves colour,
How great Nature, clearly, joys in red and green ;
    What sweet thoughts she thinks
    Of violets and pinks,
And a thousand flushing hues, made solely to be
    seen ;
    See her whitest lilies
    Chill the silver showers,
And what a red mouth has her rose, the woman of
    the flowers !

    Uselessness divinest
    Of a use the finest
Painteth us, the teachers of the end of use ;
    Travellers weary-eyed
    Bless us, far and wide ;
Unto sick and prisoned thoughts we give sudden
    truce ;
    Not a poor town window
    Loves its sickliest planting,
But its wall speaks loftier truth than Babylon's
    whole vaunting.

Sage are yet the uses
Mixed with our sweet juices
Whether man, or may-fly, profit of the balm ;
As fair fingers healed
Knights from the olden field,
We hold cups of mightiest force to give the wildest
    calm.
E'en the terror Poison
Hath its plea for blooming ;
Life it gives to reverent lips, though death to the
    presuming.

And oh ! our sweet soul-taker,
That thief the honey-maker,
What house hath he, by the thymy glen !
In his talking rooms
How the feasting fumes,
Till his gold cups overflow to the mouths of men !
The butterflies come aping ‐
Those fine thieves of ours,
And flutter round our rifled tops, like tickled
    flowers with flowers.

See those tops, how beauteous !
What fair service duteous
Round some idol waits, as on their lord the Nine ?
Elfin court 'twould seem ;
And taught perchance that dream,
Which the old Greek mountain dreamt upon
    nights divine.
To expound such wonder
Human speech avails not :
Yet there dies no poorest weed, that such a glory
    exhales not.

Think of all these treasures,
Matchless works and pleasures,
Every one a marvel, more than thought can say ;
Then think in what bright show'rs
We thicken fields and bowers,
And with what heaps of sweetness half stifle wanton
      May :
Think of the mossy forests
By the bee-birds haunted,
And all those Amazonian plains, lone lying as
      enchanted.

Trees themselves are ours ;
Fruits are born of flowers ;
Peach and roughest nut were blossoms in the spring ;
The lusty bee knows well
The news, and comes pell-mell,
And dances in the bloomy thicks with darksome
      antheming.
Beneath the very burthen
Of planet-pressing ocean
We wash our smiling cheeks in peace, a thought
      for meek devotion.

Tears of Phœbus,—missings
Of Cytherea's kissings,
Have in us been found, and wise men find them still ;
Drooping grace unfurls
Still Hyacinthus' curls,
And Narcissus loves himself in the selfish rill ;
Thy red lip, Adonis,   .
Still is wet with morning ;
And the step that bled for thee, the rosy briar
      adorning.

Oh, true things are fables,
Fit for sagest tables,
And the flowers are true things, yet no fables they;
Fables were not more
Bright, or loved of yore,
Yet they grew not, like the flow'rs, by every old
pathway.
Grossest hand can test us ;
Fools may prize us never ;
Yet we rise, and rise, and rise, marvels sweet for
ever.

Who shall say that flowers
Dress not heav'n's own bowers ?
Who its love, without them, can fancy,—or sweet
floor ?
Who shall even dare
To say we sprang not there,
And came not down that Love might bring one
piece of heav'n the more?
O pray believe that angels
From those blue dominions
Brought us in their white laps down, 'twixt their
golden pinions.

CHRISTMAS.[1]

A SONG FOR THE YOUNG AND THE WISE.

[" New Monthly Magazine," Dec. 1836. " Works,
1844, 1857, 1860. Kent, 1889. " Canterbury Poets," 1889.]

CHRISTMAS comes! He comes, he
 comes,
Ushered with a rain of plums ;
Hollies in the windows greet him ;
Schools come driving post to meet him ;
Gifts precede him, bells proclaim him,
Every mouth delights to name him ;
Wet, and cold, and wind, and dark,
Make him but the warmer mark ;
And yet he comes not one-embodied,
Universal 's the blithe godhead,
And in every festal house
Presence hath ubiquitous.
Curtains, those snug room-enfolders,
Hang upon his million shoulders.
And he has a million eyes
Of fire, and eats a million pies,
And is very merry and wise ;
Very wise and very merry,
And loves a kiss beneath the berry.

 Then full many a shape hath he,
 All in said ubiquity :

[1] Leigh Hunt wrote many papers on the subject of Christmas, which were collected in the "Manchester Weekly Times" (Supplement), Dec. 24th, 1869.—ED.

Now is he a green array,
And now an "eve," and now a "day;"
Now he's town gone *out* of town,
And now a feast in civic gown,
And now the pantomime and clown
With a crack upon the crown,
And all sorts of tumbles down;
And then he's music in the night,
And the money gotten by't:
He's a man that can't write verses,
Bringing some to ope your purses;
He's a turkey, he's a goose,
He's oranges unfit for use;
He's a kiss that loves to grow
Underneath the mistletoe;
And he's forfeits, cards, and wassails,
And a king and queen with vassals,
All the "quizzes" of the time
Drawn and quartered with a rhyme;
And then, for their revival's sake,
Lo! he's an enormous cake,
With a sugar on the top
Seen before in many a shop,
Where the boys could gaze forever,
They think the cake so very clever.
Then, some morning, in the lurch
Leaving romps, he goes to church,
Looking very grave and thankful,
After which he's just as prankful,
Now a saint, and now a sinner,
But, above all, he's a dinner;
(*Vide* Mr. Hervey's book,[1]

[1] "The Book of Christmas," by Thomas Hervey; with

And the picture of the cook)
He's a dinner, where you see
Everybody's family ;
Beef, and pudding, and mince-pies,
And little boys with laughing eyes,
Whom their seniors ask arch questions,
Feigning fears of indigestions
(As if they, forsooth, the old ones,
Hadn't, privately, tenfold ones):
He's a dinner and a fire,
Heaped beyond our hearts' desire—
Heaped with log, and baked with coals,
Till it roasts your very souls,
And your cheek the fire outstares,
And you all push back your chairs,
And the mirth becomes too great,
And you all sit up too late,
Nodding all with too much head,
And so go off to too much bed.

O plethora of beef and bliss !
Monkish feaster, sly of kiss !
Southern soul in body Dutch !
Glorious time of great Too-Much !
Too much heat, and too much noise,
Too much babblement of boys ;
Too much eating, too much drinking,
Too much ev'rything but thinking ;
Solely bent to laugh and stuff,
And trample upon base Enough ;

illustrations by R. Seymour. A manual, plump and sufficing
as the season ; the production of a spirit, companionable,
gentlemanly, and poetical.

Oh, right is thy instinctive praise
Of the wealth of Nature's ways.
Right thy most unthrifty glee,
And pious thy mince-piety !
For behold ! great Nature's self
Builds her no abstemious shelf,
But provides (her love is such
For *all*) her own great, good Too-Much,—
Too much grass, and too much tree,
Too much air, and land, and sea,
Too much seed of fruit and flower,
And fish, an unimagin'd dower !
(In whose single roe shall be   ⎫
Life enough to stock the sea—   ⎬
Endless ichthyophagy !)   ⎭
Ev'ry instant through the day
Worlds of life are thrown away;
Worlds of life, and worlds of pleasure,
Not for lavishment of treasure,
But because she's so immensely
Rich, and loves us so intensely,
She would have us, once for all,
Wake at her benignant call,
And all grow wise, and all lay down
Strife, and jealousy, and frown,
And, like the sons of one great mother,
Share, and be blest, with one another.

A HYMN TO BISHOP ST. VALENTINE.

["Monthly Repository," Feb. 1838. "Works," 1844, 1857, 1860. Kent, 1889.]

THE day, the only day returns,
The true *redde letter* day returns,
When summer time in winter burns ;
When a February dawn
Is opened by two sleeves in lawn
Fairer than Aurora's fingers,
And a burst of all bird singers,
And a shower of *billet-doux*,
Tinging cheeks with rosy hues,
And over all a face divine,
Face good-natured, face most fine,
Face most anti-saturnine,
Even thine, yea, even thine,
Saint of sweethearts, Valentine !

See, he's dawning ! See, he comes
With the jewels on his thumbs
Glancing us a ruby ray
(For he's sun and all to-day) !
See his lily sleeves ! and now
See the mitre on his brow !
See his truly pastoral crook,
And beneath his arm his book
(Some sweet tome *De Arte Amandi*):
And his hair, 'twixt saint and *dandy*,
Lovelocks touching either cheek,

And black, though with a silver streak,
As though for age both young and old,
And his look, 'twixt meek and bold,
Bowing round on either side,
Sweetly lipped and earnest eyed,
And lifting still, to bless the land,
His very gentlemanly hand.

   Hail ! oh hail ! and thrice again⎫
Hail, thou clerk of sweetest pen ! ⎬
Connubialest of clergymen !   ⎭
Exquisite bishop !—not at all
Like Bishop Bonner ; no, nor Hall,
That gibing priest ; nor Atterbury,
Although he was ingenious, very,
And wrote the verses on the "Fan ; "
But then he swore,—unreverend man !
But very like good Bishop Berkeley,
Equally benign and clerkly ;
Very like Rundle, Shipley, Hoadley,
And all the genial of the godly ;
Like De Sales, and like De Paul ;
But most, I really think, of all,
Like Bishop Mant, whose sweet theology
Includeth verse and ornithology,
And like a proper rubric star,
Hath given us a new "Calendar,"
So full of flowers and birdly talking,
'Tis like an Eden bower to walk in.
Such another See is thine,
O thou Bishop Valentine ;
Such another, but as big
To that, as Eden to a fig ;

For all the world's thy diocese, }
All the towns and all the trees, }
And all the barns and villages : }
The whole rising generation
Is thy loving congregation :
Enviable's indeed thy station ;
Tithes cause thee no reprobation,
Dean and chapter's no vexation,
Heresy no spoliation.
Begged is thy participation ;
No one wishes thee translation,
Except for some sweet explanation.
All decree thee consecration !
　　Beatification !
　　Canonization !
All cry out, with heart-prostration,
Sweet's thy text-elucidation,
Sweet, oh sweet's thy visitation,
And Paradise thy confirmation.

RONDEAU.[1]

["Monthly Chronicle," Nov. 1838. "Works," 1844,
1857, 1860. "Favourite Poems," 1877. Kent, 1889.
"Macmillan's Magazine," 1889. "Canterbury Poets,"
1839.]

JENNY kissed me when we met,
　　Jumping from the chair she sat in ;
Time, you thief, who love to get
　　Sweets into your list, put that in ;
Say I'm weary, say I'm sad,

[1] In this one case I have adopted the later reading, be-

Say that health and wealth have missed me,
Say I'm growing old, but add,
    Jenny kiss'd me.

AN ANGEL IN THE HOUSE.

[" Works," 1844, 1857, 1860.   Kent, 1889.   "Canterbury Poets," 1889.]

HOW sweet it were, if without feeble
            fright,
    Or dying of the dreadful beauteous
            sight,
An angel came to us, and we could bear
To see him issue from the silent air
At evening in our room, and bend on ours
His divine eyes, and bring us from his bowers
News of dear friends, and children who have never
Been dead indeed,—as we shall know for ever.
Alas ! we think not what we daily see
About our hearths,—angels, that *are* to be,
Or may be if they will, and we prepare
Their souls and ours to meet in happy air ;—
A child, a friend, a wife whose soft heart sings
In unison with ours, breeding its future wings.

cause it is the familiar one, and is so much happier. When
the poem first appeared in the " Monthly Chronicle" at the
end of an article on Pope, the name was "Nelly," and in
line 5 the word "jaundiced" took the place of the present
"weary." The poem was inspired by Mrs. Carlyle, who was
herself inspired to the act by hearing the sonnet "On a Lock
of Milton's Hair," printed on p. 90.—ED.

LOVER OF MUSIC TO HIS PIANO-FORTE.

[" Works," 1844, 1857, 1860.   Kent, 1889.]

H friend, whom glad or grave we seek,
    Heaven-holding shrine !
    I ope thee, touch thee, hear thee speak,
    And peace is mine.
No fairy casket full of bliss,
    Out-values thee :
Love only, wakened with a kiss,
    More sweet may be.

To thee, when our full hearts o'erflow
    In griefs or joys,
Unspeakable emotions owe
    A fitting voice :
Mirth flies to thee, and Love's unrest,
    And Memory dear.
And Sorrow, with his tightened breast,
    Comes for a tear.

Oh since few joys of human mould
    Thus wait us still,
Thrice blessed be thine, thou gentle fold
    Of peace at will.
No change, no sullenness, no cheat,
    In thee we find ;
Thy saddest voice is ever sweet,—
    Thine answer, kind.

DIRGE FOR AN INFANT.

["Cambridge Chronicle," Feb. 3rd, 1849. "Selections from British Poets," Dublin, 1858. Kent, 1890.]

HE is dead and gone—a flower
Born and withered in an hour.
Coldly lies the death-frost now
On his little rounded brow;
And the seal of darkness lies
Ever on his shrouded eyes.
He will never feel again
Touch of human joy or pain,
Never will his once bright eyes
Open with a glad surprise;
Nor the death-frost leave his brow—
All is over with him now.

Vacant now his cradle-bed,
As a nest from whence hath fled
Some dear little bird, whose wings
Rest from timid flutterings.
Thrown aside the childish rattle;
Hushed for aye the infant prattle—
Little broken words that could
By none else be understood,
Save the childless one who weeps
O'er the grave where now he sleeps.
Closed his eyes, and cold his brow—
All is over with him now!

FAITH, HOPE, AND CHARITY

ARE THE PROSPECTS OF MANHOOD.

[Printed from the manuscript formerly in possession of
Mr. Ireland.]

'TIS said that Faith declines ; believe it
    not ;
    Faith grows and spreads. Faith in the
    happier lot
Of human kind ; therefore, sweet Hope, in thee ;
And Faith in God's own climax, Charity.[1]
'Tis strange that Christians should be proud, who
    hold
Prospects in scorn, by Christ himself foretold.
What was the song sung on this blessed night,
When round the shepherds fell the golden light
That held the angel, and he said " Fear not ? "
What but the promise of that happier lot
Fit to bring angels down, as it did then
Of " peace on earth and good-will towards men?"

THE MELANCHOLY LOVER TO HIS
MISTRESS.

[Printed from the manuscript formerly in possession of
Mr. Ireland.]

OH think not that the pensive air,
    That shades thy lover's mien,
Betrays a secret, silent care
    Within this heart serene ;

[1] And now remain Faith, Hope, and Charity, but the
greatest of these is Charity."—*St. Paul.*

Bliss, just like grief, will sometimes start
In tear-drops to the eye ;
And what but bliss can reach this heart,
Sweet girl, when thou art by?

Have you not felt, when all the heart
Is big with love's excess,
A restless longing to impart
The transport you possess ?

'Tis this that o'er my gazing eyes
Thus throws a mournful hue ;
'Tis this returns in quiv'ring sighs
The love that smiles in you.

SIMILE OF BEAUTIFUL NIGHT.

LITERALLY TRANSLATED FROM HOMER.

["Examiner," June 16th, 1816.]

A S when around the moon the stars appear
Loveliest in heaven, and all is hushed
and clear,
When mountain-tops, and uplands,
bask in light,
And woods, and all th' ætherial depth of night
Seems opened back to heav'n, and sight is had
Of all the stars, and shepherds' hearts are glad ;
So many, 'twixt the ships and river, shone
The Trojan fires in front of Ilion.

SPRIGHTLY OLD AGE.

ANACREON, ODE 41.

["Examiner," March 31st, 1816.]

HEN the sports of youth I see,
Youth itself returns to me.
Then indeed my old age springs,
To the dance on starting wings.
Stop, Cybele, roses there,—
As befits a dancer's hair :
Grey-beard sloth away be flung ;
And I'll join you, young for young,
Afterwards go fetch we wine,
Bounty of a fruit divine ;
And I'll show what age can do,
Able still to warble too,
Able still to drink down sadness,
And display a graceful madness.

ROSES.

FROM ANACREON.

["Foliage," 1818.]

το ρόδον το των ερωτων.

HE rose, the flower of love,
Mingle with our quaffing ;
The rose, the lovely-leaved,
Round our brows be weaved,
Genially laughing.

O the rose, the first of flowers,
Darling of the early bowers,
   Ev'n the gods for thee have places,
Thee too Cytherea's boy
Weaves about his locks for joy,
   Dancing with the Graces.

Crown me then; I'll play the lyre,
   Bacchus, underneath thy shade;
Heap me, heap me higher and higher,
And I'll lead a dance of fire
   With a dark deep-bosomed maid.

GREEK PRETENDERS TO PHILO-SOPHY DESCRIBED.

FROM THE ANTHOLOGY.

(The original is in similar compound words.)

[" Works," 1844, 1857, 1860.]

LOFTY-brow-flourishers,
   Nose-in-beard-wallowers,
   Bag-and-beard-nourishers,
   Dish-and-all-swallowers;
Old-cloak-investitors,
   Barefoot-lookfashioners,
Night-private-feasteaters,
   Craft-lucubrationers;
Youth-cheaters, word-catchers, vaingloryosophers,
Such are such seekers of virtue, philosophers.

CUPID SWALLOWED!

A PARAPHRASE FROM THE SAME.

["New Monthly Magazine," Oct., 1836. "Works,"
1844, 1857, 1860. Kent, 1889.]

'OTHER day as I was twining
Roses, for a crown to dine in,
What, of all things, 'midst the heap
Should I light on, fast asleep,
But the little desperate elf,
The tiny traitor, Love himself!
By the wings I pinched him up
Like a bee, and in a cup
Of my wine I plunged and sank him,
And what d'ye think I did ?—I drank him.
'Faith, I thought him dead.   Not he !
There he lives with tenfold glee ;
And now this moment with his wings
I feel him tickling my heart-strings.

EPITAPH ON EROTION.

FROM MARTIAL.

["Indicator," Nov. 10th, 1819. "Works," 1832, 1844,
1857, 1860. Kent, 1889.]

NDERNEATH this greedy stone
Lies little sweet Erotion ;
Whom the Fates, with hearts as cold,
Nipped away at six years old.
Thou, whoever thou may'st be,

That hast this small field after me,
Let the yearly rites be paid
To her little slender shade ;
So shall no disease or jar
Hurt thy house, or chill thy Lar ;
But this tomb here be alone,
The only melancholy stone.

ATYS THE ENTHUSIAST.

A DITHYRAMBIC POEM TRANSLATED FROM CATULLUS.

["The Reflector," 1810.   "Foliage," 1818.]

ATYS o'er the distant waters hurried in
    his rapid bark
    Soon with foot of wild impatience
    touched the Phrygian forest
    dark,
Where amid the awful shades possessed by mighty
    Cybele,
In his zealous frenzy blind
And wand'ring in his hapless mind,
With flinty knife he gave to earth the weights that
    stamp virility.
Then as the widowed being saw its wretched limbs
    bereft of man,
And the unaccustomed blood that on the ground
    polluting ran,
With snowy hand it snatched in haste the timbrel's
    airy round on high,

That opens with the trumpet's blast, thy rites,
    Maternal Mystery ;
And upon its whirling fingers while the hollow
    parchment rung,
Thus in outcry tremulous to its wild companions
    sung :—
Now rush on, rush on with me,
Worshippers of Cybele,
To the lofty groves of the deity !
Ye vagabond herds that bear the name
Of the Dindymenian dame !
Who seeking strange lands, like the banished of
    home,
With Atys, with Atys distractedly roam ;
Who your limbs have unmanned in a desperate
    hour
With a frantic disdain of the Cyprian pow'r ;
Who have carried my sect through the sea and its
    terrors,—
Exult ye, exult in your fiercely-wrought errors !
No delay, no delay,
But together away,
And follow me up to the Dame all-compelling,
To her high Phrygian groves and her dark Phry-
    gian dwelling,
Where the cymbals they clash, and the drums
    they resound,
And the Phrygian's curved pipe pours its moan-
    ings around,
Where the ivy-crowned priestesses toss with their
    brows,
And send the shrill howl through their deity's
    house,

Where they shriek, and they scour, and they mad-
    den about,—
'Tis there we go bounding in mystical rout.

  No sooner had spoken
This voice half-broken,
When suddenly from quiv'ring tongues arose the
    universal cry,
The timbrels with a boom resound, the cymbals
    with a clash reply,
And up the verdant Ida with a quickened step the
    chorus flew,
While Atys with the timbrel's smite the terrible
    procession drew ;
Raging, panting, wild, and witless, through the
    sullen shades it broke,
Like the fierce, unconquered heifer bursting from
    her galling yoke ;
And on pursue the sacred crew, till at the door of
    Cybele,
Faint and fasting, down they sink in pale immo-
    vability :
The heavy sleep—the heavy sleep grows o'er their
    failing eyes,
And locked in dead repose the rabid frenzy lies.

  But when the Sun looked out with eyes of light
Round the firm earth, wild seas, and skies of
    morning white,
Scaring the ling'ring shades
With echo-footed steeds,
Sleep, from the suffering Atys, winged his charms
To fair Pasithaë's expectant arms,

II.   L

And the poor dreamer woke, oppressed with sad-
     ness,
To mem'ry woke and to collected madness :—
Struck with its loss, with what it was, and where,
Back trode the wretched being in despair
To the sea-shore, and stretching forth its eye
O'er the wide waste of waters and of sky,
Thus to its country cried with tears of misery :—

  My country, oh my country, parent state,
Whom, like a very slave and runagate,
Wretch that I am, I left for wilds like these,
This wilderness of snows and matted trees,
To house with shiv'ring beasts and learn their
     wants,
A fierce intruder on their sullen haunts,—
Where shall I fancy thee ? Where cheat mine
     eye
With tricking out thy quarter in the sky ?
Fain, while my wits a little space are free,
Would my poor eyeballs strain their points on
     thee !
Am I then torn from home and far away ?
Doomed through these woods to trample, day by
     day,
Far from my kindred, friends, and native soil,
The mall, the race, and wrestlers bright with oil ?
Ah wretch, bewail, bewail ; and think for this
On all thy past variety of bliss !
I was the charm of life, the social spring,
First in the race, and brightest in the ring :
Warm with the stir of welcome was my home,
And when I rose betimes, my friends would come

Smiling and pressing in officious scores,
Thick as the flowers that hang at lovers' doors :—
And shall I then a minist'ring madman be
To angry gods ?—A howling devotee ?—
A slave for Cybele to haunt and vex,—
Half of myself,—a man without a sex ?
And must I feel, unrespited of woes,
Th' o'erhanging winter of these mountain snows ?
Roam through the ghastly scene for evermore,
Skulk with the stag, and wander with the boar ?
Ah me ! Ah me ! Already I repent ;
E'en now, e'en now I feel my shame and punish-
    ment !

   As thus with rosy lips the wretch grew loud,
Startling the ears of heaven's imperial crowd,
The Mighty Mistress o'er her lion yoke
Bowed in her wrath,—and loos'ning as she spoke
The left-hand savage, scatterer of herds,
Roused his fell nature with impetuous words :—

· Fly, ruffian, fly, indignant and amain,
And scare this being, who resists my reign,
Back to the horror-breathing woods again !
Lash thee, and fly, and shake with sinewy might
Thine ireful hair, and as at dead of night
Fill the wild echoes with rebellowing fright !

   Threat'ning she spoke, and loosed the vengeance
    dire,
Who, gath'ring all his rage, and glaring fire,
Starts with a roar, and scours beneath her eyes
Scatt'ring the splintered bushes as he flies :

Down by the sea he spies the wretch at last,
And springs precipitous :—the wretch as fast,
Flies raving back into his living grave,
And there for ever dwells, a savage and a slave.

O Goddess ! Mistress ! Cybele ! dread name !
O mighty Pow'r ! O Dindymenian dame !
Far from my home thy visitations be :
Drive others mad, not me :
Drive others into impulse wild and fierce in-
    sanity !

I need not apologise to such readers as I address, for the plain-speaking in the translation of
Atys (from *Preface to " Foliage "*).

It is most probable, therefore, that Atys was
really a religious enthusiast, who mutilated himself in the hope of extinguishing his passions, and
founded a severe and fanatical sect in honour of the
mother of the gods ; and it is under this character
he is represented by Catullus . . . . as a piece of
composition nothing can be completer than the
(Latin poem's) arrangement and whole conduct : as
a piece of interest, there is no poem of the same
brevity that unites with so powerful an effect the
two great tragic requisites of pity and terror. In
the beginning all is hurry and brief execution,
followed by enthusiasm ; then after a night's sleep,
come recollection and repentance ; then returns
madness and rapidity shuts the scene ; and the
poet, in the agitation of his sympathy, concludes
with an impassioned prayer to Cybele against

similar visitations on himself." (From *Prefatory Remarks in the " Reflector."*)

ACME AND SEPTIMIUS, OR THE ENTIRE AFFECTION.

FROM CATULLUS—CARMEN XIV.

["Examiner," Sept. 13th, 1812. "Feast of Poets," &c., 1814. "Temple Bar," June, 1876.[1]]

"OH ! Acme love ! " Septimius cried,
As on his lap he held his bride,
"If all my heart is not for thee,
And doats not on thee desperately,
And if it doat not more and more,
As desperate heart ne'er did before,
May I be doomed, on desart ground,
To meet the lion in his round ! "[2]
    He said, and Love, on tiptoe near him,
    Kind at last, and come to cheer him,[3]
    Clapped his little hands to hear him.

But Acme to the bending youth
Just dropping back that rosy mouth,

[1] Where Lord Brougham's letter of approving criticism is also printed.

[2] The ancients believed that perjured persons were particularly liable to encounter wild beasts.

[3] It has been supposed that the passage here, which is rather obscurely expressed in the original, at least to modern apprehension, alludes to some difficulties with which the lovers had met, and which had hitherto prevented their union.

Kissed his reeling, hovering eyes,
And " O my life, my love ! " replies,
" So may our constant service be
To this one only Deity,
As with a transport doubly true
He thrills your Acme's being through ! "
    She said ; and Love, on tiptoe near her,
    Kind at last, and come to cheer her,
    Clapped his little hands to hear her.

Favoured thus by heaven above,
Their lives are one return of love ;
For he, poor fellow, so possessed,
Is richer than with East or West,
And she, in her enamoured boy,
Finds all that she can frame of joy.
    Now who has seen, in Love's subjection,
    Two more blest in their connection,
    Or a more entire affection ?

JOVIAL PRIEST'S CONFESSION.

FROM WALTER DE MAPES.

[" Works," 1832, 1844, 1857, 1860.]

There is already an imitation by Mr. Huddesford of the
following reverend piece of wit ; and one of the passages in it
beats anything in the present version. It is the beginning
of the last stanza—
    Mysterious and prophetic truths
      I never could unfold 'em,
    With a flagon of good wine,
      And a slice of cold ham.
The translation here offered to the reader is intended to

be a more literal picture of the original, and to retain more
of its intermixture of a grave and churchman-like style.
[The original] is preserved in the " Remains " of the learned
Camden, who says, in his pleasant way, that " Walter de
Mapes, Archdeacon of Oxford, who, in the time of King
Henry the Second, filled England with his merriments, con-
fessed his love to good liquor in this manner : "—

DEVISE to end my days—in a tavern
    drinking ;
May some Christian hold for me—the
    glass when I am shrinking ;
That the Cherubim may cry—when they see me
    sinking,   ,
God be merciful to a soul—of this gentleman's way
    of thinking.

A glass of wine amazingly—enlighteneth one's
    internals ;
'Tis wings bedewed with nectar—that fly up to
    supernals ;
Bottles cracked in taverns—have much the sweeter
    kernels
Than the sups allowed to us—in the college
    journals.

Every one by nature hath—a mould which he was
    cast in ;
I happen to be one of those—who never could
    write fasting ;
By a single little boy—I should be surpassed in
Writing so : I'd just as lief—be buried, tombed
    and grassed in.

Every one by nature hath—a gift too, a dotation :
I, when I make verses,—do get the inspiration

Of the very best of wine—that comes into the
    nation :
It maketh sermons to abound—for edification.
Just as liquor floweth good—floweth forth my
    lay so ;
But I must moreover eat—or I could not say so ;
Nought it availeth inwardly—should I write all
    day so ;
But with God's grace after meat—I beat Ovidius
    Naso.

Neither is there given to me—prophetic anima-
    tion,
Unless when I have eat and drank—yea, e'en to
    saturation ;
Then in my upper story—hath Bacchus domina-
    tion,
And Phœbus rusheth into me, and beggareth all
    relation.

SONG OF FAIRIES ROBBING ORCHARD.

FROM RANDOLPH.

From some Latin verses in the old English drama of
"Amyntas, or the impossible Dowry."

["Tatler," Sept. 8th, 1830.   "Works," 1832, 1844, 1857,
1860.   "Monthly Repository," Sept., 1837. Kent, 1889.]

WE the Fairies, blithe and antic,
    Of dimensions not gigantic,
    Though the moonshine mostly keep us
    Oft in orchards frisk and peep us.

Stolen sweets are always sweeter,
Stolen kisses much completer,
Stolen looks are nice in chapels,
Stolen, stolen be your apples.

When to bed the world are bobbing,
Then's the time for orchard robbing ;
Yet the fruit were scarce worth peeling
Were it not for stealing, stealing.[1]

FROM DANTE.

[Printed from the manuscript formerly in possession of Mr. Ireland.]

THROUGH me it goes into the Dolourous City,
    Through me, to Dolour where no end [must] be ;
Through me, to people, lost beyond all pity.
'Twas Justice moved my great creator.   Me
High Wisdom made ; and at my fashioning

---

[1] In the "Monthly Repository" appear two extra verses, which have never been reprinted.

    Now for all this store of apples,
    Laud we with the voice of chapels.
    Elves, methinks, were ordain'd solely
    To keep orchard-robbing holy.

    Home then, home ; let's recreate us
    With the maids whose dairies wait us ;
    Kissing them with pretty grapples,
    All mid junkets, wine, and apples.

Were Eldest Love, and Heavenly Potency ;
Before me was not a created thing,
If not for ay ; and ay I guard the centre.
Abandon every hope, all ye who enter.

These words, in dusky characters, did I see
Written above a gate ; at which I said,
" Master, the sense of them seems hard to see."
And he, as one prepared, looked and replied ;
"'Tis fitting here all doubt be laid aside
All poverty of spirit be as dead."

LAURA'S BOWER.

FROM PETRARCH.

["Examiner," Dec. 6th, 1816. "Works," 1832, 1844,
1857, 1860.]

CLEAR, fresh, and dulcet streams,
　　Which the fair shape who seems
　　To me sole woman, haunted at noon-
　　　　tide ;
Bough, gently interknit,
(I sigh to think of it,)
Which formed a rustic chair for her lovely side ;
And turf, and flowers bright-eyed,
O'er which her folded gown
Flow'd like an angel's down ;
And you, O holy air and hushed,
When first my heart at her sweet glances gushed ;
Give ear, give ear with one consenting,
To my last words, my last, and my lamenting.

If 'tis my fate below,
And heaven will have it so,
That love must close these dying eyes in tears,
May my poor dust be laid
In middle of your shade,
While my soul naked mounts to its own spheres.
The thought would calm my fears,
When taking, out of breath,
The doubtful step of death ;
For never could my spirit find
A stiller port after the stormy wind ;
Nor in more calm, abstracted bourne,
Slip from my travailled flesh, and from my bones
       outworn.

Perhaps, some future hour
To her accustomed bower
Might come the untamed, and yet the gentle she ;
And where she saw me first,
Might turn with eyes athirst
And kinder joy to look again for me ;
Then, oh the charity !
Seeing amidst the stones
The earth that held my bones,
A sigh for very love at last
Might ask of Heaven to pardon me the past :
And Heaven itself could not say nay,
As with her gentle veil she wiped the tears away.

How well I call to mind,
When from those boughs the wind
Shook down upon her bosom flower on flower ;
And there she sat, meek-eyed,

In midst of all that pride,
Sprinkled and blushing through an amorous shower.
Some to her hair paid dower,
And seemed to dress the curls
Queenlike, with gold and pearls ;
Some, snowing, on her drapery stopped,
Some on the earth, some on the water dropped ;
While others, fluttering from above,
Seemed wheeling round in pomp, and saying,
      " Here reigns Love."
How often then I said,
Inward and filled with dread,
" Doubtless this creature came from paradise ! "
For at her look the while,
Her voice and her sweet smile,
And heavenly air, truth parted from mine eyes ;
So that, with long-drawn sighs,
I said, as far from men,
" How came I here, and when ? "
I had forgotten ; and alas !
Fancied myself in heaven, not where I was :
And from that time till this, I bear
Such love for the green bower, I cannot rest else-
      where.

   Nov. 25th, 1816.

BEAUTY OF ALCINEA.

TRANSLATED FROM ARIOSTO ("ORLANDO FURIOSO," CANTO 7, ST. 14).

["Indicator," No. 2, Oct. 20th, 1819.]

ER bosom is like milk, her neck like
    snow ;
    A rounded neck; a bosom, where you
      see
Two crisp young ivory apples come and go,
Like waves, that on the coast beat tenderly,
When a sweet air is ruffling to and fro.

DEPRECIATION OF THE NAME OF JOHN.

FROM CASA.

["Monthly Repository," Sept., 1837. "Works," 1844, 1857, 1860.]

ERE I some fifteen years younger or
    twenty,
    Master Gandolfo, I'd unbaptize myself,
    On purpose not to be called John. I
never
Can do a single thing in the way of business,
Nor set out fast enough from my own door,
But half-a-dozen people are calling after me ;
Though, when I turn, it isn't me ; such crowds
Are issuing forth, named John, at the same
    moment.

'Tis downright insult ; a mere public scandal.
Clergymen,[1] lawyers, pedants,—not a soul,
But his name's John.   You shall not see a face,
Looking like what it is, a simpleton's—
Barber's, porkman's, or tooth-drawer's,—but the
    fellow
Seems by his look to be a John,—and *is* one !
I verily think that the first man who cried
Boiled apples or maccaroni, was a John ;
And so was he who found out roasted chestnuts,
And how to eat cucumbers, and new cheese.
By heavens ! I'd rather be a German ; nay,
I'd almost said a Frenchman ; nay, a Jew,
And be called Matthew, or Bartholomew,
Or some such beast,—or Simon.   Really people
Who christen people, ought to pause a little,
And think what they're about.—O you who love
    me,
Don't call me John, for God's sake ; or at least,
If you must call me so, call it me softly ;
For as to mentioning the name out loud,
You might as well call after one like a dog,—
Whistle, and snap your fingers, and cry " Here,
    boy."

Think of the name of John upon a title-page !
It damns the book at once ; and reasonably :
People no sooner see it, than they conclude
They've read the work before.—Oh I must say
My father made a pretty business of it,
Calling *me* John ! *me*, 'faith—his eldest son !
Heir to his—poverty ! Why there's not a writ,

[1] Casa was himself in orders, and subsequently a bishop.

But nine times out of ten, is served on John,
And what still more annoys me, not a bill :
Your promiser to pay is always John.

  Some people fondly make the word a com-
          pound,
And get some other name to stand its friend,
Christening the hapless devil John-Antony,
John-Peter or John-Charles, or John-Battista ;
There's even John-Barnard, and John-Martin !—
          Oh,
See if the other name likes his society !

  It never does, humour it as you will.
Change it, diminish it, call it Johnny, or Jacky,
Or Jack, 'tis always a sore point,—a wound ;—
Shocking, if left alone,—and worse, if touched.

ODE TO THE GOLDEN AGE.

FROM TASSO.

["Amyntas," 1820. "Indicator," March 15th, 1820.
"Works," 1832, 1844, 1857, 1860.]

IT is to be borne in mind, that the opinions expressed in
this famous ode of Tasso's, are only so expressed on the
supposition of their compatibility with a state of innocence.

LOVELY age of gold !
Not that the rivers rolled
With milk, or that the woods dropped
          honey-dew ;
Not that the ready ground
Produced without a wound,

Or the mild serpent had no tooth that slew ;
Not that a cloudless blue
Forever was in sight,
Or that the heaven which burns,
And now is cold by turns,
Looked out in glad and everlasting light ;
No, nor that even the insolent ships from far
Brought war to no new lands, nor riches worse
        than war :
But solely that that vain
And breath-invented pain,
That idol of mistake, that worshipped cheat,
That Honour,—since so called
By vulgar minds appalled,
Played not the tyrant with our nature yet.
It had not come to fret
The sweet and happy fold
Of gentle human-kind ;
Nor did its hard law bind
Souls nursed in freedom ; but that law of gold,
That glad and golden law, all free, all fitted,
Which Nature's own hand wrote—What pleases,
        is permitted.

Then among streams and flowers,[1]
The little winged Powers
Went singing carols without torch or bow ;
The nymphs and shepherds sat
Mingling with innocent chat
Sports and low whispers ; and with whispers low,
Kisses that would not go.

  [1] This verse is also given in the "Indicator," Oct. 20th, 1819, with the comment, "Honi soit qui mal y pense."

The maiden budding o'er,
Kept not her bloom uneyed,
Which now a veil must hide,
Nor the crisp apples which her bosom bore ;
And oftentimes, in river or in lake,
The lover and his love their merry bath would
  take.

'Twas thou, thou, Honour, first
That didst deny our thirst
Its drink, and on the fount thy covering set ;
Thou bad'st kind eyes withdraw
Into constrained awe,
And keep the secret for their tears to wet ;
Thou gatheredst in a net
The tresses from the air,
And mad'st the sports and plays
Turn all to sullen ways,
And putt'st on speech a rein, in steps a care.
Thy work it is,—thou shade that wilt not move,
That what was once the gift, is now the theft of
  Love.

Our sorrows and our pains,
These are thy noble gains.
But oh, thou Love's and Nature's masterer,
Thou conqueror of the crowned,
What dost thou on this ground,
Too small a circle for thy mighty sphere ?
Go, and make slumber dear
To the renowned and high ;
We here, a lowly race,
Can live without thy grace,
After the use of mild antiquity.
  II.   M

Go, let us love ; since years
No truce allow, and life soon disappears ;
Go, let us love ; the daylight dies, is born ;
But unto us the light
Dies once for all, and sleep brings on eternal
    night.

MARRIAGE À LA MODE.

FROM MASSON.

[" Tatler," Sept. 30th, 1830. " Works," 1860.]

TOM, you should take a wife—*Now love
    forbid!*
    I found you one last night.—*The devil
    you did!*
Softly ; perhaps she'll please you.—*Oh, of course!*
Fifteen.—*Alarming!*—Witty.—*Nay, that's worse!*
Discreet.—*All show!*—Handsome.—*To lure the
    fellows!*
High-born.—*Ay, haughty!*—Tender-hearted.—
    Jealous!
Talents o'erflowing,—*Ay, enough to sluice me!*
And then, Tom, such a fortune!—*Introduce me.*

LOVE AND AGE.

FROM D'HOUDETÔT.

["Liberal," No. 3, 1823. "Works," 1844, 1857, and 1860.]

WHEN young, I loved. At that delicious
  age,
    So sweet, so short, love was my sole
      delight ;
And when I reached the time for being sage,
  Still I loved on, for reason gave me right.

Age comes at length, and livelier joys depart,
  Yet gentle ones still kiss these eyelids dim ;
For still I love, and love consoles my heart ;
  What could console me for the loss of Him?

THE EXAMINER.

1808.

PROSPECTUS.

THE promises of newspapers have become almost as valuable as the .promises of courtiers. Every new journal grows vain upon its modest pretensions; the proprietors, with much unintentional simplicity, are always flattering themselves on their industry and genius; and it must be confessed, that no politics can be more impartial, no criticism more refined, and no general information given with a more literary air, than what these gentlemen intend. But all this is magnificent in its announcement only. The newspaper proves to be like the generality of its species, very mean in its subserviency to the follies of the day, very miserably merry in its puns and its stories, extremely furious in politics, and quite as feeble in criticism. You are invited to a literary conversation, and you find nothing but scandal and commonplace. There is a flourish of trumpets, and enter Tom Thumb. There is an earthquake, and a worm is thrown up.

The reader anticipates us here. "Ay," cries he, "here is the old Prospectus cant : every thing is wretched in comparison with the NEW PAPER : we shall have the ancient BUT in a minute . . . . BUT THE PROPRIETORS OF THE EXAMINER SCORN TO COME FORWARD . . . . and so forth." This is a very good observation, but a little inapplicable. The proprietors, who will be the writers of the EXAMINER, cannot entirely deceive the town, for they are in some degree already known to the public. The gentleman who till lately conducted the THEATRICAL DEPARTMENT in the News will criticise the Theatre in the EXAMINER ; and as the public have allowed the possibility of IMPARTIALITY in that department, we do not see why the same possibility may not be obtained in POLITICS.

The great error of politicians is that old fancy of SOLON, who insisted that it was infamous for a citizen to be of no party, and endeavoured by a law to make the Athenians hypocrites. This conceit not only destroys every idea of mediation between two parties, but does not even suppose that both may be wrong. Yet all history may convince us that he who resolutely professes himself attached to any party is in danger of yielding to every extreme for the mere reputation of his opinion ; he will argue for the most manifest errors of this or that statesman, because he has hitherto agreed with him—an obstinacy as stupid as if a pedestrian were to express his satisfaction with a tempest at night, because he had enjoyed sunshine in the morning.

The big and little Endians in " Gulliver " have
not yet taught us the folly of mere party ; and one
of the most ridiculous inconsistencies in the human
character is that enjoyment, which all ages have
expressed in satirical productions, without receiving
benefit from them ; they drink the physic with a
bold and pleasant countenance, and instantly prepare to counteract its effect—or, rather, every man
thinks the physic excellent for everybody but himself. "*Party*," says SWIFT, "is the madness of
many for the gain of a few."[1] When Scarmen-
tado in VOLTAIRE arrived at Ispahan, he was
asked whether he was for black mutton or white
mutton ; he replied that it was equally indifferent
to him, provided it was tender. A wise man
knows no party abstracted from its utility, or existing, like a shadow, merely from the opposition of
some body. Yet, in the present day, we are all so
erroneously sociable that every man, as well as
every journal, must belong to some class of politicians—he is either Pittite or Foxite, Windhamite,
Wilberforcite, or Burdettite ; though, at the same
time, two-thirds of these disturbers of coffee-
houses might with as much reason call themselves
Hivites, or Shunamites, or perhaps Bedlamites.

A crowd is no place for steady observation. The
EXAMINER has escaped from the throng and bustle,
but he will seat himself by the wayside, and con-
template the moving multitude as they wrangle
and wrestle along. He does not mean to be as
noisy as the objects of his contemplation, or to
abuse them for a bustle which resistance merely

[1] The motto of " The Examiner."—ED.

increases, or even to take any notice of those mis-
chievous wags who might kick the mud towards
him as they drive along ; but the more rational
part of the multitude will be obliged to him, when
he warns them of an approaching shower, or in-
vites them to sit down with him and rest themselves, or advises them to take care of their
pockets. As to the language and style in which
this advice will be given, it would be ridiculous to
promise that which haste or the head-ache might
hinder him from performing. Perhaps it must still
be left to statesmen to amuse in politics.

With respect to the THEATRIC CRITICISM, the
proprietors merely observe that it will be the same
spirit of opinion and manner with the LATE
theatrical observations in the News. The critic
trusts he has already proved in that paper that he
has no respect for error, however long established,
or for· vanity, however long endured. He will
still admire Mr. Kemble when dignified, but by
no means when pedantic ; he hopes still to be
satisfied with MR. DIBDIN in a Christmas pantomime, but is afraid he shall differ with him as to
his powers for comedy. Yet the town may be
assured, that if either Mr. Dibdin or Mr. Reynolds
should suddenly become a man of wit, the critic
will be as eager to announce the metamorphosis as
if it were the discovery of transmuting lead into
gold. Perhaps he may be considered vain in proclaiming his qualifications for criticism, but he
cannot help betraying how infinitely the dramatists
of the day have abused him. He would not have
mentioned this, but the natural infirmity of an

author, speaking of himself, must be pardoned for
once, especially when he does not dwell upon so
flattering a subject.

The little attention which newspapers pay to
the FINE ARTS is no little proof of an indifferent
taste, especially when we consider that this country
possesses its own school of painting. That we have
artists like *West*, who claim every merit so much
admired in the old masters, except, indeed, that
of being in the grave ; and that a youth, named
WILKIE, has united HOGARTH with the Dutch
school by combining the most delicate character
with the most delicate precision of drawing.
These great geniuses make us the best compensa-
tion for the loss of the drama by reviving tragedy
and comedy on the canvas. Yet they are scarcely
ever noticed except in these annual sketches of the
exhibition, which a newspaper cannot help giving,
because they constitute part of the fugitive news.
We will try, therefore, to do a little better. An
artist will conduct our department of the Fine
Arts. If he does not promise for his taste, he
promises for his industry. He will be eager in
announcing to the public not only the promiscuous
merits of exhibitions, but those individual pictures
which deserve to engage the public attention
singly, those happy rarities, which like the *Wolfe*
and *La Hogue* of *West*, and the *Village Politicians*, *Blind Fiddler*, and *Steward receiving
Rent*, of *Wilkie*, almost create æras in the history
of painting.

As it requires but a moderate portion of good
sense to regulate the DOMESTIC ECONOMY of a

newspaper, the proprietors might indulge themselves a little more, perhaps, in promising peculiar
care in this department. At any rate, they will
never acquiesce in those gayer or gloomier follies
of the world, whether of rakes or of prize-fighters,
to which the papers give their sanction with so
cold-blooded an indifference. They do not intend, like the *Society for the Suppression of Vice,*
to frighten away the innocent enjoyments of the
poor by dressing religion in a beadle's laced hat,
and praying heaven to bless the ways of informers ;
but they will never speak of adultery and seduction
with levity, nor affect to value that man, however
high his rank or profuse of interest his connection,
who dares to take advantage of his elevation in
society to trample with gayer disdain on the social
duties. As to those selfish and vulgar cowards,
whether jockies, who will run a horse to death, or
cockfighters, who sit down to a table on which
fowls are served up alive . . . . as to those miserable ruffians, whether the ornaments of a goal or
the disgracers of a noble house, who thank God for
giving them strength by endeavouring to annihilate
the strength of others, who, like a Hottentot beauty,
value themselves upon a few bones, and call fighting
for a few guineas English spirit, they are most probably out of the reach of literary ridicule, which
must be read before it is felt : but we shall use our
strongest endeavours to hold up them and their
admirers to the contempt of others who might
mistake their murderous business for manliness.
What ! shall English noblemen crowd the high-
ways to admire the exploits of a few thieves and

butchers? Shall they rush from the Court and the Senate to enrich a few sturdy vagabonds with the labour of their virtuous peasantry, to shout over a fallen brute, and to be astonished at that sublime merit which is excelled by the leg of a dray-horse? What an amiable vivacity!

We are almost afraid to say that NO ADVERTISEMENTS WILL BE ADMITTED in the EXAMINER, for this assertion generally means that they will; but the public will be inclined, perhaps, to believe the proprietors when they declare, that though they intend to be engaged in the publication of books, they will not advertise a single one of their own works. Advertisements therefore will hardly be inserted for anybody else: they shall neither come staring in the first page at the breakfast-table to deprive the reader of a whole page of entertainment, nor shall they win their silent way into the recesses of the paper under the mask of general paragraph to filch even a few lines: the public shall neither be tempted to listen to somebody in the shape of wit who turns out to be a lottery-keeper, nor seduced to hear a magnificent oration which finishes by retreating into a peruke, or rolling off into a blacking-ball.

If some weekly papers, however, have a page of Advertisements at the beginning, they have also a page of Markets at the end: they commence by informing us of the retail of London, and conclude by communicating the wholesale. This is a pleasant uniformity, especially in a paper containing all the news of the week. But as there are fifteen daily papers that present us with advertise-

ments six days in the week, and as there is perhaps about one person in a hundred, who is pleased
to see two or three columns occupied with the
mutabilities of cattle and the vicissitudes of leather,
the proprietors of the EXAMINER will have as
little to do with bulls and raw hides, as with
lottery-men and wig-makers.

Above all, the New Paper shall not be disgraced
by those abandoned hypocrites, whose greatest
quackery is their denial of being quacks. Their
vile indecency shall not gloat through the mask of
philanthropy, sickness shall not be flattered into
incurability, nor debauchery indulged to the last
gasp by the promises of instant restoration. If
the paper cannot be witty or profound, it shall at
least never be profligate.

THE EXAMINER

1808.

PREFACE.

[At end of Vol. I.]

LEGISLATORS, lovers, and journalists,
are the three divisions of men that most
hate to be reminded of their promises.
The perjuries of the first are no subject
for jesting : the second declare, that Heaven laughs
at theirs : and as to the third, I am sure that both
Heaven and earth, if the former has any thing to
do with the matter, must laugh at theirs. It is

with some pride, therefore, that the *Examiner* can close his first volume, not only with a complacent retrospect towards his prospectus, but with the approbation of those subscribers, who, as they were the first to doubt, are now the most willing to trust him.

As the good faith of the prospectus has thus been acknowledged, I need not descant here upon what its promises have already told the public. It will be allowed me, however, for that very reason, while I sketch a slight review of what has been done, to explain what I have attempted without promising : and this consists of two endeavours : first, an humble attempt, exclusive of mere impartiality in great matters, to encourage an unprejudiced spirit of thinking in every respect, or in other words, to revive an universal and *decent philosophy, with truth for its sole object*, and, second, an attempt to improve the style of what is called fugitive writing, by setting an example of, at least, a *diligent respect for the opinion of literary readers.*

I. . . . Mere impartiality, with respect to men, that is, an indifferent repose amidst political bustle, will not teach us to be patriots, though it may hinder us from being placemen. We must shake off all our indolence, whether positive or negative, whether of timidity or of negligence, we must shake off all our prejudices, and look about us ; and in this effort we must be assisted by philosophy.

And let us neither be alarmed by the name of philosophy, because it has been degraded by little

men, nor overawed, because it has been rendered
arduous by great. ` Let us regard it in its original
and etymological sense, as a love of wisdom, and
not in its acquired and ornamental, as an attainment of it. The essence of philosophy is the
cultivation of common reason, ... Freedom from
party spirit is nothing but the love of looking
abroad upon men and things, and this leads to
universality, which is the great study of philosophy, so that the true love of inquiry and the love
of one's country move in a circle. This is the
"zeal according to knowledge," which I would be
an humble instrument of recommending.

II. The ignorance and corruption of the journals
naturally produced a correspondent style. The
jarring spirit of past years seemed to have de-
stroyed every political refinement both of speaking
and writing. Graceful persuasion forsook the
Senate ; wit and argument the press. The newspapers, occupied with momentary rumour and in-
vective, appeared to have no leisure for anything
becoming ; and as the sounds of speech are affected
by a deranged constitution, the whole public voice
grew vulgar as it grew violent. People are now
beginning to change their tone in these matters ;
but even now, when every other species of literature has gained at least an elegant mediocrity, the
progress of periodical style has scarcely reached
correctness ; and it is remarkable that those
papers which are the most politically corrupt, are
still the most corrupt in everything else. It becomes a public writer, therefore, to show the company his intellect keeps, and to attempt a language

worthy of the sentiments he feels, and the country
for which he writes.   If a true style consists of
" proper words in proper places," the definition is
indisputable in political discussion, which ought to
be the vehicle of the clearest and purest ideas.
What concerns everybody should be universally
intelligible, though at the same time it should be
written with a care for ornament, and it is for
these reasons, that while I have avoided as much
as possible the quotation of languages in politics,
in order that everybody might be able to read me,
I have not hesitated to employ what little
pleasantry I could, in order that everybody might
wish to read me.

There is very little political writing in the
daily papers, and their articles are read throughout, because they are short, as well as of daily and
party interest ; but I have ever remarked that in
the political essays of the weekly prints, the interest of the reader has been proportional to the
manner as well as matter of the writing.   It is the
same in theatrical criticism, a department which
none of the papers seems inclined to dispute with
a person fond of the subject, the daily ones for
want of independence, and the weekly for want of
care. . . . Little miscellaneous sketches of character and manners have been introduced into the
Examiner, as one small method of habituating
readers to general ideas of the age.   The Fine
Arts also have met with an attention proportion-
able to their influence and national character, as
well as to their rapid improvement in this country.
Their improvement, indeed, is at once an honour

and a disgrace to the nation, for it is the sole work of individuals. *The politicians and the government have not yet acquired the art, which they must acquire, of looking about them with enlarged eyes, and fighting the great enemy with his only good weapon, and his only real glory, the cultivation of the human intellect. . . .*

On their resolution to proceed as they have begun, the proprietors say little. It is in the place where their country is—at the bottom of their hearts.

OF THE EXAMINER.

FROM "EXPLANATION AND RETROSPECTION" —THE "EXAMINER" TWENTY YEARS AGO.

["Monthly Repository," Oct. 1837.]

IT was the Robin Hood of its cause, plunder excepted ; and by the gaiety of its daring, its love of the green places of poetry, and its sympathy with all who needed sympathy, produced many a brother champion that beat it at its own weapons. Hazlitt, in its pages, first made the public sensible of his great powers. There Keats and Shelley were first made known to the lovers of the beautiful. There Charles Lamb occasionally put forth a piece of criticism, worth twenty of the editor's, though a value was found in those also ; and there we had the pleasure of reading the other day one of the earliest addresses to the public of a great man, who, with a hand mighty with justice, succeeded in lifting up a nation into the equal atmosphere, which all have a right to breathe,—Daniel O'Connell. Let no friend, who ever mentions our having suffered for a "libel" (a word we hate) on the Prince Regent, forget to add, that it was occasioned by the warmth of our sympathy with that nation, and our anger at seeing the Prince break his promises with it.

THE REFLECTOR.

PROSPECTUS.

OF all pieces of fiction, the most amiable and the least interesting are Prospectuses. The reader, who in his love of inquiry, used to catch at every new opportunity of being amused and instructed, has been so often disappointed in this way, that he is prepared to resist every thing in the shape of a promise ; and, in fact, the more ardent the promise, the colder becomes his incredulity. In vain the Prospectus comes before him on the most advantageous terms and softest paper : in vain, like the scheme of a lottery, it sets in array its gigantic types to catch his eye, and make him pay for treasures he will never realize : in vain the writer promises him all sorts of intellectual feasts, research the most various and profound, a style the most pithy and accomplished, and poetry, in one word, original. He recognizes the old story ;

he anticipates at once, in the composition before him, all the beauties of the style, the poetry, and the research :—in short, he crumples up the paper, and forgets the writer as quickly as he does the street-herald, who insinuates into your hand the merits of a pair of boots, or the attracting qualities of a monster.

In presenting, therefore, a new Magazine to the notice of the Public, the Proprietors are not at all inclined, either by their pride or their interest, to take such infallible means of rendering it ridiculous. The REFLECTOR will be an attempt to improve upon the general character of Magazines, and all the town knows, that much improvement of this kind may be effected without any great talent. Reform of periodical writing is as much wanted in Magazines, as it formerly was in Reviews, and still is in Newspapers. It is true, there are still to be found some agreeable and instructive articles in the Magazines—a few guineas thrown by richer hands into the poor's box :—indolent genius will now and then contribute a lucky paragraph, and should inquiry have no better place of resort, it will scarcely fail of a *brief* answer from among a host of readers. But the field is either given up to the cultivation of sorry plants, or it is cut up into a petty variety of produce to which every thing important is sacrificed. It is needless to descant on the common lumber that occupies the greater portion of these publications—on the want of original discussion ; or the recipes for and against cooking and coughing ; or the stale jests ; or the plagiarisms ; or the blinking pettiness of antiquarianism,

II.   N

which goes toiling like a mole under every species
of rubbish, and sees no object so stupendous as an
old house or a belfry ; or lastly, on the quarrels
between Verax and Philalethes, who fight for
months together upon a straw, and prove at last,
to the great edification of the reader, that neither
is to be believed.—The old Magazines are no-
toriously in their dotage ; and as to the new ones,
that have lately appeared, they have returned to
the infancy of their species—to pattern-drawing,
doll-dressing, and a song about Phillis.   These
flimsy publications, though unworthy of notice in
themselves, are injurious to the taste of the town
in more than one respect, inasmuch as they make
a show of employing the Arts, while they are only
degrading and wasting them.   Their principal
feature is *superb embellishment*, otherwise called
unique, splendid, and *unrivalled* ; that is to say,
two or three coloured plates of fine ladies and
fashions, hastily tricked up by some unfortunate
engraver, who, from want of a better taste in the
country, is compelled to throw away his time and
talents upon these gorgeous nothings.   To suit the
style of the ornamental part, the literary presents
you with a little fashionable biography ; some remarks at length on eating, drinking or dressing ;
an anecdote or two ; a design or two for hand-
kerchiefs and settees ; a country-dance ; a touch
of botany, a touch of politics, a touch of criticism ;
a faux pas ; and a story *to be continued*, like those
of the Improvisatori, who throw down their hats
at an interesting point and must be paid more to
proceed.   The *original poetry* need not be de-

scribed : of all the antiquities of a Magazine, this is the most antique,—a continual round of sad hours, of lips, darts, and epitaphs, of sighings *Ah why!* and wonderings *Ah where!*

It is thus, that in the best as well as worst Magazines, you see a multiplicity of trifles taking place of all that is most important in the *character of the times*—that character, which, as it is the most useful feature, ought also to be the most prominent and most engaging feature in this species of publication. A Magazine should properly be a *Chronicle for posterity*, but what will posterity care for our queries upon wooden legs, and our squabbles upon a turnip? And what will it think of the intellect of an age, which in the midst of so many and such mighty interests could be content with a trifling so frivolous?

These are faults easily avoided by such as have the least regard for the age and its reputation ; and to avoid the grosser faults of Magazines will be the first aim, perhaps the best recommendation, of the REFLECTOR.—One of its first cares will be *Politics*, which the Magazines generally dismiss in crude and impatient sketches. Politics, in times like these, should naturally take the lead in periodical discussion, because they have an importance and interest almost unexampled in history, and because *they are now, in their turn, exhibiting their reaction upon literature, as literature in the preceding age exhibited its action upon them.* People, fond of books, and of the gentler arts of peace, are very apt to turn away from politics as from a barren and fearful ground, productive of nothing

but blood-stained laurels ; they see there, no
doubt, the traces of the greatest misery and folly ;
but if they look a little more narrowly, they will
see also the seeds of the most flourishing and re-
freshing arts. What such men neglect from dis-
taste, less minds neglect from regarding politics in
too common, too every-day a light, and in our own
age, we have seen a whole nation, which has been
called " thinking," gradually lose the habit of
looking out upon the times at large, because it has
been occupied with a thousand petty squabbles and
interests. This is a fault, which as it is one of the
most fatal to political character, a writer should be
most earnest to deprecate. It becomes us all to
philosophize as much as possible in an age, when
human intellect, opposed to *human weakness,* has
been called so unobstructedly into play, and has
risen so fearfully into power. Each number of the
REFLECTOR will contain, besides a Retrospect of
the Quarterly Events, an Essay or two upon Domestic or Foreign Policy ; and in ascending from
particulars to generals, it will endeavour to view
the times in that *historical* light, which striking in
broad and centrical masses, and not wasting itself
on the corners and detail of the picture, gives pro-
minence, clearness, and effect to the principal objects. Its opinions will be exactly those of the
Examiner, speaking freely of all parties without
exception, attached most strongly to the Constitution in letter and in spirit, and for that single
reason most anxious for Reform. The Editor
speaks of his independence in this matter without
fear of rebuff, not only because he knows not a

single politician personally, and is conscious of having as undisturbed opinions on the subject as he has upon the theatre or the weather, but because the readers of the *Examiner* have acknowledged the consistency of that paper, and he has had the good fortune to make the most infamous writers in town his enemies. The only piece of interest he shall solicit for the REFLECTOR, is to recommend it to those gentlemen as a work, which he trusts will be worthy of their unqualified abuse and most ferocious patronage.

In *Theatrical Criticism*, the Magazines, generally speaking, have always been the unambitious and unthinking followers of the Daily Papers; and personal interest is of so active and social a disposition that it always finds means to corrupt a trading spirit, equally petty in its views of reputation. It is true, the Newspapers themselves at last begin to be ashamed of praising writers who have become bye-words for nonsense, and they dismiss the subject, if not with their former panegyrics, with a flippant indulgence half-ashamed of itself. But this style is utterly unworthy of a subject so important to the manners and literary character of a nation, and serves no purpose but to expose the critic, and make the very dramatists despise him. The Editor of the REFLECTOR, occupied in another work with exposing the grinning monsters that are every day given to the world as representations of nature, does not intend to particularize so much in the Magazine :—he will do his best to review the quarterly theatricals in their general character, with less of minute, but more of comparative and didactic criticism. The theatres, in their proper state, afford a most instructive as well as amusing course of lessons to a cultivated nation, not, as their enemies insinuate, because they pretend to teach morals better than religion itself, but because they exhibit our virtues in social action and instruct us in that kind of wisdom, which, without being worldly-minded, is so adapted to keep us in proper harmony with the world. But occupied as they have been for years past with mere caricature, they obtain neither the social nor the sentimental end of the drama, they shew us neither what we are nor what we ought to be. A person wishing to be profited by modern comedy, might amuse and edify himself just as well by making all sorts of faces in a looking-glass. When SHAKESPEARE appears now and then in the list of performances, he looks like a sage in a procession of merry-andrews, and is suffered to pass by with little more than a cold respect. He carries too great an air of truth, and does not make people laugh enough. This is the more to be lamented, since a taste for the drama is never so easily and entirely vitiated, as when self-love is left undisturbed to its frivolous enjoyments, when advice thinks only how it shall appear ridiculous, and satire grows powerless from neglecting its real objects. The better part of the town have acquired sense enough to despise these things, critically speaking, but if they still continue to be amused by them, they will only be despised in their turn, as one of the dramatists plainly hinted the other day in a preface. You may hold a fool in a contemptible light, but when you condescend to laugh and be on a level with him, he is more than even with your contempt.

The *Fine Arts* are in a very different state from the Drama, and demand a different mode of treatment. The latter is in its second infancy with all the vices of a frivolous dotage, and must, if possible, be ground young again :—the former are in their first infancy and must be handled more tenderly, though at the same time with no vicious indulgence. The Proprietors need not descant on the want of all ardour upon this head in our periodical works. It is said that the country at present has no notion of a taste for art ; and WINCKELMANN, who from continually contemplating the southern sunshine, seems to have looked upon us with spots before his eyes, said that it always did and always would want a taste, from the nature of its climate. He forgot that our poets have never been surpassed ; that Paris, which was the focus of literary taste, is in the same latitude with Tartary ; and that Athens is situate beneath a fickle sky. There are, no doubt, several obstructions in the way of modern art, and among them, however trivial it may appear at first sight, the constrained and concealing style of modern dress is a formidable hindrance to the attainment of a noble and familiar mastery of form. But these disadvantages have become common to all Europe. A fine climate, an enlivening sunshine, an atmosphere, free and lucid, through which objects become pictures, may certainly dispose the mind to its own enjoyment, and the fancy to an undisturbed leisure of creation ; and from this circumstance it is likely, that taste and a love of genius will be more *diffused* among warm countries than others. But there are minds that are above all circumstances of this kind in regard to genius, and there will be always a sufficient number of such minds in an *intellectual nation*, if they exert themselves as they ought, and call forth the public attention. It is *government*—not easy or happy government in particular, but government of a disposition to patronize, or of a nature to rouse emulation, that has the greatest influence in these matters. In fact, how came WINCKELMANN himself, a Prussian by birth and education, to be the most enthusiastic, some say the best, connoisseur of his time? Or how is it that Flanders has produced better painters than all the south of Europe, Italy excepted? Or how is it again, that the Arabs, the Persians, and all the most refined Eastern nations, have never produced a single painter? Man may be the slave of error, of political circumstance, or of himself; but none but a few hypochondriacs are the slaves of clouds and weather-glasses. The British, it must be confessed, have at present no very great love for the arts; but, nevertheless, they have a much greater than formerly. There was a time when Italy herself wanted taste: it was created by a few great artists, and so it must be in other countries, just as poets and not critics create rules and a taste for poetry. Patronage is generally languid in its birth, and if it does not easily spring up, it must be forced by genius itself. This is the idea a young artist should always have of patronage and of the means of obtaining

it. Since WINCKELMANN's time, his assertion
has been disproved, in the best way, by the reputations of REYNOLDS, BARRY, WILSON, and
WEST, the Fathers of the English school of painting. These celebrated men have laid a noble
foundation, and every thing calls upon their suc-
cessors to finish the structure—the example already
set them, the promise afforded by themselves, the
encouraging dawn of public patronage, and the
rivalry of the French nation, whom we must endeavour to conquer with mind, now that we see it
cannot be done with money.

The Editor has enlarged on these three subjects,
because the first is of most immediate importance,
and the two others require most immediate care.
They will by no means, however, occupy the
largest part of the work, the principal feature of
which will be *Miscellaneous Literature,* consisting
of Essays on Men and Manners, Enquiries into
past and present Literature, and all subjects relative to Wit, Morals, and a true Refinement.
There will be no direct Review of Books, but new
works, as far as they regard the character of the
times, will meet with passing notice; and occasional articles will be written to shew the peculiar
faults or beauties, injuriousness or utility, of such
as have strongly attracted the public attention. In
order to obtain proper room for this variety, the
REFLECTOR will consist entirely of Original
Articles, written purposely for the work, to the
exclusion of unnecessary matter, of plagiarisms
from Newspapers and Reviews, and of long extracts from books of the day. The Editor will

never be tempted to supply the deficiencies of matter, or to serve the purposes of literary quacks, by such letters as, " Sir, permit me to recommend to the notice of your *impartial* and *enlightened* readers,"or,—" Mr. Editor,—Sir, allow me through the medium of your *invaluable* Miscellany," &c. &c. These are the first tricks to be reformed, both on the side of Editor and Correspondent, as tending to degrade the true spirit of literature. Not a page will be wasted on market-prices, or stock-prices, or accounts of the weather, or histories of fashion, or obituaries that give a few weeks' renown for so many shillings. Hides and velvet-collars have, it is true, their rise and fall as well as kingdoms, but then they have distinct interests of their own, and should be left to their respective professors :—the REFLECTOR is determined not to show its ignorance on the subject, and will deviate neither into patterns, nor whip-clubs, nor portraits of "public characters," nor, in short, into any "embellishments" whatever, but such as may be supplied by the wit and knowledge of its Correspondents. The trifles of an age have undoubtedly their connection, sometimes too great a one, with its general character, and they may be handed down as a part of the portrait, just as our ancestors come down to us in their ruffles and periwigs; but the best artists are not those who attend most to these decorations; the true spirit of the likeness is in the man himself—in his air and attitude—and in the mind that looks out of his general aspect.—In a word, it is this *mind*, which the REFLECTOR will endeavour to pourtray; and the Proprietors will spare no industry, the only talent for which they can vouch, to delineate and to call forth the proper expression in those features of the age, which regard its present interests with mankind and its future character with posterity.

☞ [1]

THE INDICATOR. No. 1.

OCTOBER 13TH, 1819.

IT is the object of this periodical work to notice any subjects whatsoever within the range of the editor's knowledge or reading. He will take them up as they happen to suggest themselves, and endeavour to point out their essence to the reader, so as at once to be brief and satisfactory. The subjects will chiefly consist of curious recollections of biography; short disquisitions on men and things; the most interesting stories in history or fiction told over again, with an eye to their proper appreciation by unvulgar minds; and now and then a few original verses. Indeed, the whole matter, whatever the subject may be, will be strictly original, in one sense of the word; and it will be the editor's aim, as well as a part of his own pleasure, to render it all as entertaining as he can. To the unvulgar he exclusively addresses himself; but he begs it to be particularly understood that in this description of persons are to be included all those who, without having had a classical education,

[1] The signature frequently adopted by L. H.—the "Indicative hand."—ED.

would have turned it to right account; just as all those are to be excluded who, in spite of that "discipline of humanity," think ill of the nature which they degrade, and vulgarly confound the vulgar with the uneducated.

The Indicator will attend to no subject whatsoever of immediate or temporary interest. His business is with honey in the old woods. The editor has enough to agitate his spirits during the present eventful times, in another periodical work[1]; and he is willing to be so agitated: but as he is accustomed to use his pen, as habitually as a bird his pinion, and to betake himself with it into the nests and bowers of more lasting speculations, when he has done with public ones, he is determined to keep these haunts of his recreation free from all noise and wrangling, both for his own pleasure and for those who may chuse to accompany him.

The Indicator will appear every Wednesday morning, at an hour early enough for the breakfast-table; and though the subjects will not be temporary or those of the moment, they will be written as much at the moment as if they were; so that there will still be a certain freshness of intercourse between the editor and his readers.

[2] There is a bird in the interior of Africa, whose habits would rather seem to belong to the interior of Fairy-land: but they have been well authenticated. It indicates to honey-hunters, where the

[1] The "Examiner."—Ed.
[2] The following passage was originally printed as a heading to the "Indicator."—Ed.

nests of wild bees are to be found. It calls them
with a cheerful cry, which they answer ; and on
finding itself recognized, flies and hovers over a
hollow tree containing the honey. While they are
occupied in collecting it, the bird goes to a little
distance, where he observes all that passes ; and
the hunters, when they have helped themselves,
take care to leave him his portion of the food.—
This is the CUCULUS INDICATOR of Linnæus,
otherwise called the Moroc, Bee Cuckoo, or Honey
Bird.

> "There he arriving round about doth flie,
> And takes survey with busie, curious eye :
> Now this, now that, he tasteth tenderly."
>
> SPENSER.

DIFFICULTY OF FINDING A NAME FOR A WORK OF THIS KIND.

Never did gossips, when assembled to deter-
mine the name of a new-born child, whose family
was full of conflicting interests, experience half the
difficulty which an author finds in settling the title
for a periodical work. There is generally some
paramount uncle, or prodigious third cousin, who
is silently understood to have the chief claims, and
to the golden lustre of whose face the clouds of
hesitation and jealousy gradually give way. But
these children of the brain have no godfather at
hand : and then their single appellation is bound to
comprise as many public interests, as all the Christian names of a French or a German prince. It is
to be modest : it is to be expressive : it is to be
new : it is to be striking : it is to have something
in it equally intelligible to a man of plain under-

standing, and surprising for the man of imagination :—in one word, it is to be impossible.

How far we have succeeded in the attainment of this happy nonentity, we leave others to judge. There is one good thing however which the hunt after a title is sure to realize ;—a good deal of despairing mirth.   We were visiting a friend the other night, who can do anything for a book but give it a title ; and after many grave and ineffectual attempts to furnish one for the present, the company, after the fashion of Rabelais, and with a chair-shaking merriment which he might have joined in himself, fell to turning a hopeless thing into a jest.   It was like that exquisite picture of a set of laughers in Shakespeare :—

> " One rubbed his elbow, thus ; and fleered, and swore,
> A better speech was never spoke before :
> Another, with his finger and his thumb,
> Cried ' Via ! We will do't, come what will come !'
> The third he capered, and cried, ' All goes well !'
> The fourth turned on the toe, and down he fell.
> With that they all did tumble on the ground,
> With such a zealous laughter, so profound,
> That in this spleen ridiculous, appears,
> To check their laughter, passion's solemn tears."
> *Love's Labour's Lost.*

Some of the names had a meaning in their absurdity, such as the Adviser, or Helps for Composing ;—the Cheap Reflector, or Every Man His Own Looking-Glass ;—the Retailer, or Every Man His Own Other Man's Wit ;—Nonsense, To be Continued.   Others were laughable by the mere force of contrast, as the Crocodile, or Pleasing Companion ;—Chaos, or the Agreeable Miscel-

lany ;—the Fugitive Guide ;—the Foot Soldier, or
Flowers of Wit ;—Bigotry, or the Cheerful In-
structor ;—the Polite Repository of Abuse ;—
Blood, being a Collection of Light Essays. Others
were sheer ludicrousness and extravagance, as the
Pleasing Ancestor ; the Silent Remarker ; the
Tart ; the Leg of Beef, by a Layman ; the Inge-
nious Hatband ; the Boots of Bliss ; the Occasional Diner ; the Tooth-ache ; Recollections of a
Very Unpleasant Nature ; Thoughts on Taking up
a Pair of Snuffers ; Thoughts on a Barouche-Box ;
Thoughts on a Hill of Considerable Eminence ;
Meditations on a Pleasing Idea ; Materials for
Drinking ; the Knocker, No. I. ;—the Hippopo-
tamus Entered at Stationers' Hall ; the Piano-
forte of Paulus Æmilius ; the Seven Sleepers at
Cards ; the Arabian Nights on Horseback :—with
an infinite number of other mortal murders of
common sense, which rose to "push us from our
stools," and which none but the wise or good-
natured would ever think of laughing at.

THE LIBERAL.

[1822.]

E are not going to usher in our publication with any pomp of prospectus. We
mean to be very pleasant and ingenious, of course ; but decline proving
it beforehand by a long commonplace. The
greater the flourish of trumpets nowadays, the

more suspicious what follows. Whatever it may be our luck to turn out, we at least wave our privilege of having the way prepared for us by our own mouth-pieces,—by words with long tales, and antitheses two and two. If we succeed, so much the better. If not, we shall at all events not die of the previous question, like an honest proposal in Parliament.

But we are forced to be prefatory, whether we would or no, for others, it seems, have been so anxious to furnish us with something of this sort, that they have blown the trumpet for us, and done us the honour of announcing, that nothing less is to ensue than a dilapidation of all the outworks of civilized society. Such at least they say is our intention, and such would be the consequences if they, the trumpeters, did not take care by counter-blasts, to puff the said outworks up again. We should be more sensible of this honour if it did not arise from a confusion of ideas. They say that we are to cut up religion, morals, and everything that is legitimate—a pretty carving. It only shows what they really think of their own opinions on those subjects. The other day a ministerial paper said that "robes and coronations were the strong-holds of royalty." We do not deny it; but if such is their strength, what is their weakness? If by religion they meant anything really worthy of divine or human beings; if by morals they meant the only true morals, justice and beneficence; if by everything legitimate, they meant but half of what their own laws and constitutions have pro-vided against the impudent pretensions of the

despotic,—then we should do our best to leave
religion and morals as we found them, and show
their political good faith at least half as much respect as we do.   But when we know,—and know
too from our intimacy with various classes of
people,—that there is not a greater set of hypocrites in the world than these pretended teachers
of the honest and inexperienced part of our
countrymen—when we know that their religion,
even when it is in earnest on any point (which is
very seldom), means the most ridiculous and un-
tenable notions of the DIVINE BEING, and in all
other cases means nothing but the Bench of
Bishops ;—when we know that their morals consist
for the most part in a secret and practical contempt
of their own professions, and for the least and best
part, of a few dull examples of something more
honest, clapped in front to make a show and a
screen, and weak enough to be made tools against
all mankind ;—and when we know, to crown all,
that their "legitimacy," as they call it, is the
most unlawful of all lawless and impudent things,
tending, under pretence that the whole world are
as corrupt and ignorant as themselves, to put it at
the mercy of the most brute understandings among
them—men by their very education in these pretensions, rendered the least fit to sympathise with
their fellow-men, and as unhappy, after all, as the
lowest of their slaves—when we know all this,
and see nine-tenths of all the intelligent men in
the world alive to it, and as resolved as we are to
oppose it, then indeed are we willing to accept the
title of enemies to religion, morals, and legitimacy,

II.   O

and hope to do our duty with all becoming pro-
faneness accordingly. God defend us from the
piety of thinking him a monster! God defend us
from the morality of slaves and turncoats, and
from the legitimacy of half-a-dozen old gentlemen,
to whom, it seems, human nature is an estate
in fee.

The object of our work is not political, except
inasmuch as all writing now-a-days must involve
something to that effect, the connection between
politics and all other subjects of interest to mankind having been discovered, never again to be
done away. We wish to do our work quietly, if
people will let us,—to contribute our liberalities in
the shape of poetry, essays, tales, translations,
and other amenities, of which kings themselves
may read and profit, if they are not afraid of seeing
their own faces in every species of inkstand.
Italian literature in particular will be a favourite
subject with us; and so was German and Spanish
to have been till we lost the accomplished scholar
and friend[1] who was to share our task, but perhaps
we may be able to get a supply of the scholarship,
though not of the friendship. It may be our good
fortune to have more than one foreign correspondent, who will be an acquisition to the reader.
In the meantime we must do our best by ourselves; and the reader may be assured he shall
have all that is in us, clear and candid at all
events, if nothing else, for

> We love to pour out all ourselves as plain
> As downright SHIPPEN or as old MONTAIGNE.

[1] Shelley, no doubt.—ED.

There are other things in the world besides kings, or even sycophants. There is one thing in particular with which we must help to bring the polite world acquainted, which is NATURE. Life really does not consist, entirely, of clubs and ball-rooms, of a collar made by Wilkins, and of the west end of the town. We confess we have a regard for the Dandies, properly so called, not the spurious race who take their title from their stays, we mean the pleasant and pithy personages who began the system, and who had ideas as well as bibs in their head. But it was on that account we liked them, because they partook of the ETHERIDGES and SUCKLINGS of old ; and why were the ETHERIDGES and SUCKLINGS better than their neighbours, but because they inherited from Old Mother Wit as well as Mother West-End, and partook of the prerogatives of Nature ? We have a regard for certain modern Barons, as well as those who got the Great Charter for us ; but is it for those who would keep, or for those who would give up the charter ? Is it for those who identify themselves with every feeble King John, or for those who have some of "GOD ALMIGHTY's Nobility " in them as well as their own ? Assuredly for the latter,—assuredly for those who have something in them "which surpasses show," and which the breath of a puffing and blowing legitimate cannot unmake.

Be present then, and put life into our work, ye spirits, not of the GAVESTONES and the DESPENSERS, but of the JOHN O'GAUNTS, the WICKLIFFES, and the CHAUCERS ;—be present, not the

slaves and sycophants of King Henry the Eighth
(whose names we have forgotten) but the HENRY
HOWARDS, the SURREYS, and the WYATTS ;—be
present, not ye other rapscallions and "booing"
slaves of the court of King JAMIE, but ye BUCHA-
NANS and ye WALTER RALEIGHS ;—be present,
not ye bedchamber lords, flogging boys, and
mere soldiers, whosoever ye are, from very Lord
THINGUMEE in King Charles's time, down to the
immortal Duke of WHAT'S-HIS-NAME now flourishing, but the HERBERTS, the HUTCHINSONS, the
LOCKES, the POPES, and the PETERBOROUGHS ;—
be present, not ye miserable tyrants, slaves, bigots,
or turncoats of any party, not ye LAUDS or ye
LAUDERDALES, ye Legitimate Pretenders (for so
ye must now be called), ye TITUS OATESES,
BEDLOWS, GARDINERS, SACHEVERELLS, and
SOUTHEYS ; but ye MILTONS, and ye MARVELLS,
ye HOADLEYS, ADDISONS, and STEELES, ye
SOMERSES, DORSETS, and PRIORS, and all who
have thrown light and life upon man, instead of
darkness and death; who have made him a thing of
hope and freedom, instead of despair and slavery ;
a being progressive, instead of a creeping creature
retrograde ;—if we have no pretensions to your
genius, we at least claim the merit of loving and
admiring it, and of longing to further its example.

We wish the title of our work to be taken in its
largest acceptation, old as well as new,—but
always in the same spirit of admiring and assisting, rather than of professing. We just as much
disclaim any assumption in it before the wise, as
we disclaim any false modesty before all classes.

All we mean is that we are advocates of every species of liberal knowledge, and that, by natural consequence in these times, we go the full length in matters of opinion with large bodies of men who are called LIBERALS. At the same time, when we say the full length, we mean something very different from what certain pretended Liberals, and all Illiberals, will take it to be ; for it is by the very reason of going to that length, in its most liberal extreme—"Ay, ay," interrupts some old club-house Gentleman, in a buff waistcoat and red face,—"Now you talk sense. Extremes meet. *Verbum sap.* I am a Liberal myself, if you come to that, and devilish liberal I am. I gave for instance five guineas out of the receipts of my sine-cure to the Irish sufferers ; but that is between ourselves. You mean, that there are good hearty fellows in all parties, and that the great business is to balance them properly ;—to let the people talk, provided they do no harm, and to let Governments go on as they do, have done, and will do for ever. Good,—good. I'll take in your journal myself ;—here's to the success of it ;—only don't make it too violent, you rogues ;—don't spoil the balance. (God ! I've spilt my bumper !) Cut up SOUTHEY as much as you please. We all think him as great a coxcomb as you do, and he bores us to death ; but spare the king and the ministers and all that, particularly Lord CASTLEREAGH and the Duke of WELLINGTON. D——d gentlemanly fellow, CASTLEREAGH, as you know, and besides he's dead. Shocking thing—shocking. It was all non-sense about his being so cold-hearted, and doing

Ireland so much harm.   He was the most gentlemanly of men.   Wars must be carried on; Malthus
has proved that millions must be slaughtered from
time to time.   The nonsense about that is as stupid
as the cry about the game-laws and those infernal
villains the poachers, who ought to be all strung up
like hares: and as to Ireland, it is flying in the
face of Providence to think that such horrible
things could happen there, and be prevented by
earthly means,—*earthly* means, sir.   Lord CASTLE-
REAGH himself referred us to Providence in all these
unavoidable matters, and he was right;—but to
think of his cutting his own throat—Good God!
so very gentlemanly a man, and in the height of
his power!   It is truly shocking! As to WELLING-
TON, he's not so gentlemanly a man certainly;
but then neither is CANNING, if you come to that.
He cannot make speeches, I own; but nor can
the king or my lord MARYBOROUGH, or a hundred
other eminent characters, and he does not make
such cursed awkward blunders as poor CASTLE-
REAGH used to do.   He has not got a very wise
look, they say; but—I don't know,—it's soldier-
like, I think; and if you come to that, what a
strange fellow old BLUCHER looked, and SUWAR-
ROW, and all those; and between ourselves, ·the
reigning monarchs are a set of as common-looking
gentry, as you'd wish to see in a summer's day; so
I don't know what people would have.   No—no—
you really mustn't speak against WELLINGTON.
Besides, he prosecutes."

We beg the reader's pardon in behalf of our
worthy interrupter.   Whatever may be his right

estimation of his friends, we need not say that he
misinterprets our notions of liberality, which certainly consist neither in making the sort of confusion, or keeping the sort of peace, which he speaks
of. There are, if he pleases, very silly fellows to
be found on both sides, and these may be good
enough to be made tools of by the clever ones; but
to confound all parties themselves with one another, which is the real end of these pretended
liberalities, and assume that none of them are a
jot better or worse than the other, and may contain just as good and generous people,—this is to
confound liberality with illiberality, narrow views
with large, the instincts of a selfish choice with
those of a generous one, and in the best and most
imposing instances, the mere amenities and ordinary virtues of private life (which may be only a
graceful selfishness, unless they go farther) with the
noblest and boldest sympathies in behalf of the
human race. It is too late in the day to be taken
in with this kind of cant; even by the jolliest of
placemen in all the benevolence of his bumpers.
The Duke of WELLINGTON is a great officer,
"after his kind." We do not mean at court,
where he is a very little officer, and condescends to
change his Marshal's staff for the stick of a Lord in
Waiting. But he is a good hunting captain,—a
sort of human setter. We allow him all his praise
in that respect, and only wish he had not confounded the rights of nations with those of a
manor. What does he mean, too, by treating
public meetings with contempt? And above all,
what did he mean by that extremely odd assump-

tion of the didactic, about teaching "a great moral
lesson?" As to Lord CASTLEREAGH, he was one
of the most illiberal and vindictive of statesmen, if
we must use that word for every petty retainer,
whom a bad system swells for a time into a part of
its own unnatural greatness. Look at his famous
Six Acts! Look at his treatment of BONAPARTE,
his patronage of such infamous journals as *the
Beacon*, his fondness for imprisoning, and for what
his weak obstinacy calls his other strong measures.
But he is dead, and people are now called upon to
be liberal! Let us be so, in God's name, in the
general sense we have of the infirmities of human
nature; but it is one thing to be liberal in behalf
of the many, and another thing to be exclusively so
in behalf of the few. Have the consequences of
Lord CASTLEREAGH's actions died with him? Are
the Six Acts dead? Are thousands of the Irish
living? We will give a specimen of the liberality
of these new demanders of liberality. The other
day, when one of the noblest of human beings,
PERCY SHELLEY, who had more religion in his
very differences with religion than thousands of
your church-and-state men, was lost on the coast
of Italy, the *Courier* said, that "Mr. PERCY
SHELLEY, *a writer of infidel poetry*, was drowned."
Where was the liberality of this canting insinua-
tion? Where was the decency, or, as it turned
out, the common sense of it? Mr. SHELLEY's
death by the waves was followed by Lord CASTLE-
REAGH's by his own hand; and then the cry is for
liberal construction! How could we not turn
such a death against the enemies of Mr. Shelley,

if we could condescend to affect such a moment's agreement with their hypocrisy? But the least we can do is to let these people see that we know them, and to warn them how they assail us. The force of our answers will always be proportioned to the want of liberality in the assailant. This is a liberality, at all events, upon which our readers may reckon. The rest, which we were going to say, is this;—that although we condemn by wholesale certain existing demands upon our submission and credulity, we are not going to discover every imaginative thing even in a religion to be nonsense, like a semi-liberalized Frenchman ; nor, on the other hand to denounce all levity and wit to be nonsense and want of feeling, like a semi-liberalized German. If we are great admirers of VOLTAIRE, we are great admirers also of GOETHE and SCHILLER. If we pay homage to DANTE and MILTON, we have tribute also for the brilliant sovereignties of ARIOSTO and BOCCACCIO.

Wherever, in short, we see the mind of man exhibiting powers of its own, and at the same time helping to carry on the best intentions of human nature—however it may overdo the matter a little on this side or on that, or otherwise partake of the common frailty through which it passes,—there we recognize the demi-gods of liberal worship;—then we bow down, and own our lords and masters ;— there we hope for the final passing away of all obscene worships, however formalized, of all monstrous sacrifices of the many to the few, however "legitimized" and besotted.

THE CHAT OF THE WEEK.

JUNE 5TH, 1830.

PROSPECTUS.

THE publication, here announced, has been suggested by the popularity of those departments in the Newspapers which are devoted to miscellaneous intelligence, and which generally consist of paragraphs equally short and amusing. Many a reader, who cares little for politics, is willing to have as much as an Editor can give him of entertaining paragraph ; and those who care for any subject in particular, or for all subjects, would willingly have them divested of what is stale and unprofitable, just as they like to have their lettuces served up without the outer leaves. Now it will be our business to get rid of the outer leaves of everything, and to serve up the heart and soul of it.

It is not our intention to be always as short as the *chat* or *multum in parvo* of a newspaper ; but as our object is to omit nothing that is of interest, and to retain nothing that is dull, our paragraphs, for the most part, will be shorter than otherwise.[1] We have no limits as to subjects. We shall take the whole round of observation—the State, the Drama, the New Publications, New Music, Man-

[1] The reader will smile to see how little we have kept our word on this point ; but we trust he will not be dissatisfied. The truth is, we were not prepared to meet with so many articles, at once so long and so interesting.

ners and Customs, the Town, the Country, the
"Great World" (meaning a place about three
miles long), and the Little World (that is to say,
all the rest of the Globe). If the word *Chat* be
thought too humble for some of our pages, it will
be an objection we shall be very glad to hear of.
Nevertheless there are few things in this world
better than real good chat, plainly so called. We
shall be happy, if what we write ourselves shall
be thought to belong to it. Higher honours will
be willingly conceded to those from whom we
extract.

The plan of our pamphlet is this. There will
be an *Original Article* at the head of it, *on the
principal subject of interest that has occurred during
the week.* This will be followed by a compilation
of the best passages in the newspapers, relating to
Politics, the *Houses of Parliament, etc. :* not whole
articles (unless the matter is of great interest
throughout), but the best passages out of articles,
as well as any separate paragraphs that may strike
us. If we meet with an article, for instance,
which contains but one striking passage, or which,
however good throughout, contains but one passage that is suitable to our purpose, *that* passage
only we select. It will be the same with regard
to *Theatricals*, which come next in order—to the
Fine Arts—to *New Books*, and so on, concluding
with the *Miscellaneous* Department, which will be
most abundant of any. To such of the paragraphs
as suggest remarks of our own, we shall append
them by way of comment ; so that the publication
may be described, in general, as a compendium of

all topics of public interest, with an original article at the head of it, and *occasional notes throughout,* the whole putting the reader in possession, at the least expense, and in the most entertaining manner, of the *Facts, Opinions,* and *Clever Sayings* of the week.

When we say that we shall retain nothing that is dull, it is not true in the absolute sense of the word ; for we shall sometimes quote a foolish author. But as extremes meet, and as we shall quote no dulness but such as is very exquisite, and nonsense that it would be difficult to match, the effect will be as good as wit. Besides, justice will thus be done to all parties. Nothing will be omitted that is convertible to the reader's pleasure ; he will see what we can go through for his sake ; and the man who was as dull as a Directory in his own pages, will find himself entertaining in ours.

We think it proper to declare, at the same time, that we shall not force this involuntary agreeableness upon anybody who does not take upon himself to dictate to the public in bad taste, or with an unworthy spirit. Neither shall we be tempted to expose anyone, dull or otherwise, who speaks in his own name, and is not to be ranked among that numerous and unprincipled class of persons who infect the high roads of Literature of the present day, and have been well characterized as "fellows with crape over their faces." If it fall in our way to notice any of these persons, and we know their names, by name they will be noticed. Our own names will always be forthcoming to such as have a right to demand them ; and, behaving like honest men ourselves, we shall respect the claims of none but the honest. Candour and merit will never be without our good word ; neither will an honourable enemy be confounded with a dishonourable. We desire no favour ourselves, if we do not show ourselves capable of doing justice to the merits of all parties, enemies as well as friends.

And now, gentle reader, if thou dost not like this very candid, intelligent, and courteous statement (all epithets belonging, time immemorial to thyself), if thou dost not take our New Publication with thy tea, or thy dessert, or thy cigar, or thy next good resolution, or with the paper which thou takest already (provided thou art rich enough to have two), "Why," as Falstaff says, "thou art not the man we took thee for." Certainly thou art not like one of us : for we plainly confess our attachment to the good things of other people, and should have liked nothing better than a work of the same sort from other hands, if we had not taken it upon our own.

THE TATLER.

SEPT. 4TH, 1830.

TO THE READERS OF THE CHAT OF THE WEEK.

E have taken an illustrious title for our new paper ; but we are not vain enough to be modest on that score, or deprecate comparison with the original possessor.   There is nothing in the humbler nature of our work to provoke it.   We borrow the title simply because the journal, called the SPECTATOR, has led the way to this adoption of a popular name ; and because in availing ourselves of the example, and being of ripe years enough to choose a clan and a god-father, we prefer the one whose name we are fondest of.   If we are not ill-natured, not insincere, and not without an eye to the common good in what may seem to be the most personal of our hostilities, the original would not be ashamed of us.

Our first number is a specimen of what THE TATLER is generally intended to be.   It will consist of entertaining extracts from books with occasional criticism ; of theatrical criticism, written with a love of the subject, and an impartiality, for which we shall claim credit at once, from a reputation for honesty in those matters ; of a miscellaneous department for stray passages of any kind ; and of any light original articles that may suggest themselves, in prose or verse, and which may be thought suitable to a breakfast-table. The paper will be published the first thing in the morning, with the newspapers of the day, to which we venture to hope it may not be found an unsuitable companion. Orders should be given for it to the regular newsmen. The town will thus have, for the first time these many years, a regular daily paper devoted to literature and criticism; and readers will be reminded of old times and names by the aspect of it. *Poins* had one thing in common with the Prince of Wales: "their legs were both of a thickness." The reader who takes up this paper, and is interested in the title of it, must be informed, that its size and general aspect is that of the original TATLER published in 1709; such as Pope and Addison held in their hands, and that Belinda bent over while the Sylphs were fanning her coffee.

LEIGH HUNT'S LONDON JOURNAL.

[April 2nd, 1834.]

ADDRESS.

THE object of this Publication, which is devoted entirely to subjects of miscellaneous interest, unconnected with politics, is to supply the lovers of knowledge, with an *English* weekly paper, similar in point of size and variety, to *Chambers's Edinburgh Journal*, but with a character a little more southern and literary. The acuteness and industry of the

writers of the *Edinburgh Journal* are understood to
have obtained a very large demand for their work ;
the illustrated information of the *Penny Magazine*,
with its admirable woodcuts, has obtained for it one
still more stupendous ; and though we may not be
able to compete with either of these phenomena,
and indeed, are prepared to be content with a sale
of reasonable enormity, yet there still remain gaps
in the supplies of public intellect, which its custo-
mers would willingly see filled up; and one of
these we propose to accommodate.   It may briefly
be described as consisting in a want of something
more connected with the *ornamental part of utility*,
—with the art of extracting pleasurable ideas from
the commonest objects, and the participations of a
scholarly experience.   In the metropolis there are
thousands of improving and enquiring minds, capable of all the elegancies of intellectual enjoyment,
who, for want of education worthy of them, are deprived of a world of pleasures, in which they might
have instructed others.   We hope to be read by
these.   In every country town there is always a
knot of spirits of this kind, generally young men,
who are known, above others, for their love of
books, for the liberality of their sentiments, and
their desire to be acquainted with all that is going
forward in connection with the graces of poetry
and the fine arts.   We hope to have *these* for our
readers.   Finally, almost every village has its cot-
tagers of a similar tendency, who, notwithstanding
their inferior opportunities, have caught from stray
pieces of poetry and fiction, a sense of what their
nature requires, in order to elevate its enjoyments

or to console its struggles; and we trust we shall become the friends of these. In a word (without meaning to disparage our excellent contemporaries, whose plans are of another sort, and have been most triumphantly borne out by success), as . the *Edinburgh Journal* gives the world the benefit of its knowledge of business, and the *Penny Magazine* that of its authorities and its pictures, so the *London Journal* proposes to furnish ingenuous minds of all classes, with such help as it possesses towards a share in the pleasures of taste and scholarship. For to leave no class unspecified, it is not without the hope of obtaining the good-will of the highest of the well-educated, who love the very talk on such subjects, as they do that of a loving friend, apart from any want of his information, and who have been rendered too wise by their knowledge not to wish well to speculations which tend to do justice to all men, and to accompany the "march of intellect" with the music of kind thoughts.

It is proposed, as the general plan of the Journal, but not without the power of change or modification, as circumstances may suggest, that it should consist of one original Paper or Essay every week, from the pen of the Editor; of matter combining entertainment with information, selected by him in the course of his reading, both old and new; of a weekly abstract of some popular or otherwise interesting book, the spirit of which will be given *entire*, after the fashion of the excellent abridgments in *Johnstone's Edinburgh Magazine;* and lastly, of a brief current notice of the Existing State of Poetry, Painting, and Music, and a general sprinkle of Notes, Verses, Miscellaneous Paragraphs, and other helps to pleasant and companionable perusal.

FURTHER REMARKS ON THE DESIGN OF THIS JOURNAL. POOR RICH MEN AND RICH POOR MEN. A WORD OR TWO ON THE PERIODICAL WRITINGS OF THE EDITOR.[1]

PLEASURE is the business of this Journal: we own it: we love to begin it with the word: it is like commencing the day (as we are now commencing it) with sunshine in the room. Pleasure for all who can receive pleasure; consolation and encouragement for the rest; this is our device. But then it is pleasure like that implied by our simile, innocent, kindly, we dare to add, instructive and elevating. Nor shall the gravest aspects of it be wanting. As the sunshine floods the sky and the ocean, and yet nurses the baby buds of the roses on the wall, so we would fain open the largest and the very least sources of pleasure, the noblest that expands above us into the heavens, and the most familiar that catches our glance in the homestead. We would break open the surfaces of habit and indifference, of objects that are supposed to contain nothing but so much brute-matter, or commonplace utility, and show what treasures they conceal. Man has not yet learned to enjoy the world he lives in; no, not the hundred-thousand-millionth part of it; and we would fain help him to render it productive of still greater joy, and to

[1] Reprinted in "The Seer."

delight or comfort himself in his task as he proceeds. We would make adversity hopeful, prosperity sympathetic, all kinder, richer, and happier. And we have some right to assist in the endeavour, for there is scarcely a single joy or sorrow within the experience of our fellow-creatures which we have not tasted ; and the belief in the good and beautiful has never forsaken us. It has been medicine to us in sickness, riches in poverty, and the best part of all that ever delighted us in health and success.

There is not a man living perhaps in the present state of society,—certainly not among those who have a surfeit of goods, any more than those who want a sufficiency,—that has not some pain which he would diminish, and some pleasure, or capability of it, that he would increase. We would say to him, let him be sure he can diminish that pain and increase that pleasure. He will find out the secret, by knowing more, and by knowing that there is more to love. " Pleasures lie about our feet." We would extract some for the unthinking rich man out of his very carpet (though he thinks he has already got as much as it can yield) ; and for the unthinking or unhoping poor one, out of his bare floor.

"Can you put a loaf on my table ? " the poor man may ask. No : but we can show him how to get it in the best manner, and comfort himself while he is getting it. If he can get it not at all, we do not profess to have even the right of being listened to by him. We can only do what we can, as his fellow-creatures, and by other means,

towards hastening the termination of so frightful
an exception to the common lot.

" Can you rid me of my gout, or my disrelish of
all things?" the rich man may ask. No: nor
perhaps even diminish it, unless you are a very
daring or a very sensible man ; and if you are very
rich indeed, and old, neither of these predica-
ments is very likely. Yet we would try. We are
inextinguishable friends of endeavour.

If you had the gout, however, *and were Lord
Holland*, you would smile and say, "Talk on."
You would suspend the book, or the pen, or the
kindly thought you were engaged in, and indul-
gently wait to see what recipes or amusing fancies
we could add to your stock.

Nay, if you were a kind of starving Dr. Johnson, who wrote a letter one day to the editor of
the magazine to which he contributed, signing
himself, "Dinnerless,[1]" you would listen to us
even without a loaf on your table, and see how far
we could bear out the reputation of the Lydians,
who are said to have invented play as a resource
against hunger. But Dr. Johnson knew he had
his remedy in his wits. The wants of the poor in
knowledge are not so easily postponed. With
deep reverence and sympathy would we be understood as speaking of them. A smile, however
closely it may border upon a grave thought, is not
to be held a levity in us, any more than sun be-

---

[1] *Impransus.* It might mean simply, that he had not
dined ; but there is too much reason to believe otherwise.
And yet how much good and entertainment did not the
very necessities of such a man help to produce us.

twixt rain. One and the same sympathy with all things fetches it out.

But to all but the famished we should say with the noble text, "Man does not live by bread alone." "A man," says Bacon, in words not unworthy to go by the side of the others, "is but what he knoweth." "I think," said Descartes; "therefore I am." A man has no proof of his existence but in his consciousness of it, and the return of that consciousness after sleep. He is therefore, in *amount* of existence, only so much as his consciousness, his thoughts, and his feelings amount to. The more he knows, the more he exists; and the pleasanter his knowledge, the happier his existence. One man, in this sense of things, and it is a sense proved beyond a doubt (except with those merry philosophers of antiquity who doubted their very consciousness, nay, doubted doubt itself), is infinitely little compared with another man. If we could see his mind, we should see a pigmy; and it would be stuck perhaps into a pint of beer, or a scent-bottle, or a bottle of wine; as the monkey stuck Gulliver into the marrow-bone. Another man's mind would show larger; another larger still: till at length we should see minds of all shapes and sizes, from a microscopic body to that of a giant or a demigod, or a spirit that filled the visible world. Milton's would be like that of his own archangel. "His stature reached the sky." Shakespeare's would stretch from the midst of us into the regions of "airy nothing," and bring us new creatures of his own making. Bacon's would be lost into the next

ages. Many a "great man's" would become invisible; and many a little one suddenly astonish
us with the overshadowing of its greatness.

Men sometimes, by the magic of their knowledge, partake of a great many things which they
do not possess : others possess much which is lost
upon them.   It is recorded of an *exquisite*, in one
of the admirable exhibitions of Mr. Mathews,
that being told, with a grave face, of a mine of
silver which had been discovered in one of the
London suburbs, he exclaimed, in his jargon, "A
mine of *sil-vau!* Good *Gaud!* You don't tell me
so!   A mine of *sil-vau;* Good *Gaud!* I've often
seen the little boys playing about, but I had no
idea that there was a mine of *sil-vau.*"

This gentleman, whom we are to understand as
repeating these words out of pure ignorance and
absurdity, and not from any power to receive information, would be in possession, while he was
expressing his astonishment at a thing unheard of
and ridiculous, of a hundred real things round
about him, of which he knew nothing.   Shakespeare speaks of a man who was "incapable of
his own distress ; " that is to say, who had not the
feelings of other men, and was insensible to what
would have distressed everybody else.   This *dandy*
would be incapable of his own wealth, of his own
furniture, of his own health, friends, books, gardens ; nay of his very hat and coat, except inasmuch as they contributed to give him one single
idea ; to wit, that of his *dandyism*.   From all
those stores, small and great, nothing but that
solitary and sorry impression would he receive.

Of all which his wealth could procure him, in the shape of a real enjoyment of poetry, paintings, music, sculpture, and the million of ideas which they might produce, he would know nothing.

Of all the countries that produced his furniture, all the trades that helped to make it, all the arts that went to adorn it, all the materials of which it was composed, and the innumerable images of men, lands, faculties, substances, elements, and interesting phenomena of all sorts to which the knowledge might give rise, he would know nothing.

Of his books he would know nothing, except that they were bound, and that they *caust* a great deal.

Of his gardens he would know nothing, except that they were "tedious," and that he occasionally had a pink out of them to put in his button-hole—provided it was the fashion. Otherwise pinks are "vulgar." Nature's and God's fashion is nothing.

Of his hat and his coat it might be thought he must know something; but he would not, except as far as we have stated;—unless, indeed, his faculties might possibly attain to the knowledge of a "fit" or a "set," and then he would not know it with a grace. The knowledge of a good thing, even in the least matters, is not for a person so poorly educated—so worse than left to grow up in an ignorance unsophisticate. Of the creatures that furnished the materials of his hat and coat,— the curious handicraft beaver, the spinster silk-worm, the sheep in the meadows (except as

mutton), nothing would he know, or care, or receive the least pleasurable thought from.　In the
mind that constitutes *his* man—in the amount of
his existence—terribly vacant are the regions—
bald places in the map—deserts without even the
excitement of a storm.　Nothing lives there but
himself—a suit of clothes in a solitude—emptiness
in emptiness.

Contrast a being of this fashion (after all allow-
ance for caricature) with one who has none of his
deformities, but with a stock of ideas such as the
other wants.　Suppose him poor, even struggling,
but not unhappy; or if not without unhappiness,
yet not without relief, and unacquainted with the
desperation of the other's ennui.　Such a man,
when he wants recreation for his thoughts, can
make them flow from all the objects, or the ideas
of those objects, which furnish nothing to the
other.　The commonest goods and chattels are
pregnant to him as fairy tales, or things in a pantomime.　His hat, like Fortunatus's Wishing Cap,
carries him into the American solitudes among the
beavers, where he sits in thought, looking at them
during their work, and hearing the majestic whispers in the trees, or the falls of the old trunks that
are repeatedly breaking the silence in those wilder-
nesses.　His coat shall carry him, in ten minutes,
through all the scenes of pastoral life and mechanical, the quiet fields, the sheep-shearing, the
feasting, the love-making, the downs of Dorset-
shire and the streets of Birmingham, where if he
meet with pain in his sympathy, he also, in his
knowledge, finds reason for hope and encourage-

ment, and for giving his manly assistance to the common good. The very toothpick of the *dandy*, should this man, or any man like him meet with it, poor or rich, shall suggest to him, if he pleases, a hundred agreeable thoughts of foreign lands, and elegance and amusement,—of tortoises and books of travels, and the comb in his mistress's hair, and the elephants that carry sultans, and the real silver mines of Potosi, with all the wonders of South American history, and the starry cross in its sky; so that the smallest key shall pick the lock of the greatest treasures; and that which in the hands of the possessor was only a poor instrument of affectation, and the very emblem of indifference and stupidity, shall open to the knowing man a universe.

We must not pursue the subject further this week, or trust our eyes at the smallest objects around us, which, from long and loving contemplation, have enabled us to report their riches. We have been at this work now, off and on, man and boy, (for we began essay-writing while in our teens,) for upwards of thirty years: and excepting that we would fain have done far more, and that experience and suffering have long restored to us the natural kindliness of boyhood, and put an end to a belief in the right or utility of severer views of any thing or person, we feel the same as we have done throughout; and we have the same hope, the same love, the same faith in the beauty and goodness of nature and all her prospects, in space and in time; we could almost add, if a sprinkle of white hairs in our black would allow us, the same

youth; for whatever may be thought of a consciousness to that effect, the feeling is so real, and
trouble of no ordinary kind has so remarkably
spared the elasticity of our spirits, that we are often
startled to think how old we have become, compared with the little of age that is in our disposition : and we mention this to bespeak the reader's
faith in what we shall write hereafter, if he is not
acquainted with us already. If he is, he will no
more doubt us than the children do at our fire-side.
We have had so much sorrow, and yet are capable
of so much joy, and receive pleasure from so many
familiar objects, that we sometimes think we
should have had an unfair portion of happiness, if
our life had not been one of more than ordinary
trial.

The reader will not be troubled in future with
personal intimations of this kind ; but in commencing a new work of the present nature and
having been persuaded to put our name at the top
of it, (for which we beg his kindest constructions,
as a point conceded by a sense of what was best
for others,) it will be thought, we trust, not unfitting in us to have alluded to them. We believe
we may call ourselves the father of the present
penny and three-halfpenny literature,—designa-
tions, once distressing to "ears polite," but now no
longer so, since they are producing so many valuable results, fortunes included. The first number of
the new popular review, the " Printing Machine,"
in an article for the kindness and cordiality of
which we take this our best opportunity of expressing our gratitude, and can only wish we could

turn these sentences into so many grips of the hand
to show our sense of it,—did us the honour of
noticing the " Indicator " as the first successful
attempt (in one respect) to revive something like
the periodical literature of former days.   We followed this with the "Companion," lately republished in connection with the " Indicator ; " and a
few years ago, in a fit of anxiety at not being able
to meet some obligations, and fearing we were
going to be cut off from life itself without leaving
answers to still graver wants, we set up a half-
reviewing, half-theatrical periodical, under the
name of the " Tatler," (a liberty taken by love,) in
the hope of being able to realize some sudden as
well as lasting profits ! So little, with all our zeal
for the public welfare, had we found out what was
so well discerned by Mr. Knight and others, when
they responded to the intellectual wants of the
many. However, we pleased some readers, whom
it is a kind of prosperity even to rank as such ; we
conciliated the good-will of others, by showing
that an ardent politician might still be a man of no
ill-temper, nor without good-will to all ; and now,
once more setting up a periodical work, entirely
without politics, but better calculated, we trust,
than our former ones to meet the wishes of many
as well as few, we are in hearty good earnest,
the public's very sincere and cordial friend and
servant,

˙LEIGH HUNT.

Union of the "London Journal" and the "Printing Machine."

On Saturday, June 6, at Mr. Knight's, 22, Ludgate Street, by the speciallest of all licenses (and the most reasonable) to wit, their own, will be married the parties above-mentioned; after which, the happy couple will set off for all parts of the world, and pass four thousand nine hundred and sixty honeymoons, such being, by the most moderate computation, the term of their natural lives.

Yes, dear Reader, the London Journal is about to "change its condition:"—not itself, observe; for why should it? It will never be more itself than at this moment; as a married journal ought to be. It only changes, or rather enriches, its condition, its relative circumstances; and being a paper, it naturally marries a printing-machine; and its partner, being a machine of the most unmechanical and intelligent description, is to be very generous and amiable, and accommodate its humours to it in so charming a manner, that there would be an end of its having any will of its own, if the two wills did not thus become one, and merge will into pleasure. And thus what a happy pair shall we be; and how glad our ninety-nine thousand hosts will be to see us every Saturday morning, like some immortal and ubiquitous Monsieur and Madame Dacier, clubbing their stocks of scholarship, and presenting themselves in all those quarters at once, chatting and to chat, and with hands full of flowers, after the fashion of those

groups on the old curtains, in which the same
identical shepherd and shepherdess are reiterated
through the whole district of chintz !

But marriage is expensive ; and we are very
much of the honest opinion of that custom in
Wales, by which young couples are set up in life
by the joint contributions of their friends, the
favours to be returned on the like occasion ; so, in
a like beautiful spirit of reciprocity, we plainly
tell our loving Readers, that they must assist us,
and prepare themselves for a magnanimous rise in
the estimation of our worth, to the value of One
Halfpenny ;—with this difference, however, from
the Welsh state of the case—that the benefit to be
received from us in return is not prospective, but
immediate, and that our halfpennyworth of increased attraction and entertainment will have
evinced a modesty (not to mince the matter) as-
tonishing, in rating its value so low.—To drop the
metaphor, and state the case simply to the readers
both of the LONDON JOURNAL and the PRINTING
MACHINE, we would have them consider, that
such as have already taken in both those papers,
and therefore paid four-pence halfpenny for the
two, may now have the essence of both for less
than half the money, and that such as have only
taken in one, may now have two instead of one,
at the least possible increase of price in one case,
and a great lowering of it in the other. The worth
of each paper will be augmented, we conceive, by
concentration,—none of the best matter of either
being lost, and none of doubtful value being required in order to fill up ; so that here will be the

LONDON JOURNAL at its old price, with the
PRINTING MACHINE added to it *for a halfpenny* ;
or the PRINTING MACHINE at two-thirds its old
price with the LONDON JOURNAL added to it *for
nothing !* It does not become us to deal in notes
of admiration, and statements of our own merits ;
but we should like some eloquent third party,—
Mr. Robins, for instance, to have this matter to
expatiate on, in some candid pulpit, or long and
just advertisement. We fancy we see the TALL
CAPITALS and BRILLIANT ADVANTAGES rearing
their heads at intervals amidst the exuberant set-
out, like the Pagoda in Kew Gardens, or the mi-
narets of some Eastern paradise ; and if he entered
thoroughly into our merits, and did really set out
the allurements of all our Gardens, fabulous and
real, and of the stories told in them, and the great
men beheld in them, and the light thrown by the
sunbeams upon their minutest flowers and pebbles,
we ask, with an emphatic but tranquil modesty,
where *would* he stop ? He would be obliged to
have a whole ' Times ' or ' Chronicle ' to himself,
—the news of the day coming in at the close of
the last column, in a brief paragraph ;—lamenting,
that it can " barely allude to interesting intelligence from Paris,"—" but the IMPORTANT ADVER-
TISEMENT "——

We *have* heard it whispered, we must confess,
in one or two quarters, that there may be some
possible peril in raising the price of our Journal,
even so small a sum, considering how many new
readers there are now-a-days, of such publications,
struggling with unfitting poverty ; but we have

reason to doubt whether we have many readers so poor as the doubt supposes, whatever be the narrowness of means which they contrive to square with the demands of intellectual thirst and hunger ; and readers of *that* kind we have no fear of losing. It has even happened to us, that Correspondents have advised us to raise our price, before we had any such grounds for it as at present ; and an intelligent and long-established book-seller, who gave us the same advice, said "Depend upon it, that readers who take in such a paper as the LONDON JOURNAL, must like it for the liberal opinions it recommends, and are not the men to part company with it for a halfpenny."

The readers of the London Journal, all rising in a body, and speaking with a soul of loving indignation at the doubt. Believe him, sir; believe him.

Readers of the Printing Machine, rising also. And are we to be doubted? Has not the Printing Machine abounded in contempt of sordidness?

Here the Editor makes a bow to innumerable faces, right and left of him; and endeavours to maintain a becoming aspect, between his natural indifference to pence, and his acquired sense of their value, and gratitude for regard.

In sober truth, we hope this junction of the two papers will be as acceptable to our friends, as it is pleasant to ourselves. The LONDON JOURNAL has long desired to be helped and enriched by other regular contributors. And in this case the Editor will be assisted in point of time, labour, and materials, not only by additional contributions, but by having a large and distinct portion of the united work placed under the responsible management of the gentleman who has edited the PRINTING MACHINE from its commencement. If the separate responsibilities were not so defined as they are in this instance, still we should have no apprehension of any collision of opinion. We are not strangers; and upon all the great principles by which the opinions and feelings of men are determined, we have as perfect an agreement as can be expected from those who hold the right of thinking for themselves, with the most hearty toleration of the thoughts of others. Nor will the Editor of THE LONDON JOURNAL omit a single contribution of his own; the old original articles, and the Romances of Real Life, Fine Arts, &c., will appear as usual, none the worse for an arrangement which may be of very serious benefit to himself; and as circumstances tend to show every day, that more good can be done to all parties by publications rather miscellaneous than critical, Mr. Knight gladly takes occasion of throwing one paper into the other, and the writers of the PRINTING MACHINE as gladly avail themselves of their briefer, and more concentrated columns, to confine their notices in future to books of the most interesting description exclusively, the nuts and sweetmeats of the tribe.

About five Pages will be devoted to the LONDON JOURNAL, and its usual variety of matter; about three to the review of books, constituting the PRINTING MACHINE. And if good spirits, plenty of subjects, and cordial co-operation, can do any-

thing towards making our paper better than before, we confidently reckon upon its being so.

. The Reader will observe that our day of
publication is changed from Wednesday to Saturday. We confess we take leave of the old day
with a pang, partly for old acquaintance sake (in
the ' Indicator' and ' Tatler '), and partly because
Charles Lamb (whose praise warrants us in being
venturous enough to repeat it) said that the former
of those publications made

" Wednesday the sweetest in the week."

(We are afraid we are guilty of a great piece of
egotism here, but the recollection of the man must
excuse it.) The reason however why we make the
change is, that Saturday turns out to be the most
convenient and profitable day for publication.
Readers of cheap periodical papers, for the most
part, find the close of the week the most convenient time for reading them,—making them part
of their Sabbath recreation (let us add, no profane
part, considering the uses and beauties of God's
creation which they set forth) ; and the vendors of
such papers, which are mostly published on the
Saturday, crowd for them accordingly towards° the
close of the week, like people to a fair, and are
apt, naturally enough, to look upon a call on their
time and attention, on less customary days, as a
supererogation which considerate editors might
spare them. We propose, therefore, in future, to
fall in with the crowd of comforts and conveniences
at the end of the week, and become a part of its
repose, and leisure, and contemplative enjoyment.

II.   Q

We hope we shall be thumbed horribly, and carried about in pockets, like a love-letter, or other certificate of merit.

LEIGH HUNT'S JOURNAL.

EDITOR'S ADDRESS TO THE READER.

HEALTH AND A HAPPY CHRISTMAS TO ALL OUR READERS! OLD AND NEW. To the old, for the sake of " Auld Lang Syne ; " and to the new, whether old or young, in the hope that they may continue to be as young of heart ; which is the reward, it seems, of such as remain constant to a certain kind of journalism.

Requested by my associates in this publication to give it the name which it bears, and thus, in a manner, personally reappearing as a journalist, it might be thought, perhaps, less modest than assured, if I entered abruptly on my task, and made no allusion to the circumstance. Kindest greetings, then, to all right good souls as aforesaid ; and may I be half as welcome to them, as they will be to me !

I confess that I would rather not have had the title of the paper identified with my name ; but the feeling which makes me do so, is, I fear, a sophistication or conventionalism, not worth attending to ; one that, with so many good examples to warrant me, I ought to be ashamed of : and, accordingly, I am so. At all events, it is a trifle

not worth saying more about. The object of the
paper is another matter. There are great changes
coming in the world; great modifications of the
best things in it, and new leave-takings, I hope,
of the worst. So thinks and hopes every body
who thinks at all. So intimated Prince Albert to
the citizens of London in the best speech ever
made by a prince in this country; adding, that he
"conceived it to be the duty of every educated
person closely to watch and study the time in
which he lives, and, as far as in him lies, to add
his humble mite of individual exertion to further
the accomplishment of what he believes Providence
to have ordained."

Now the object which I have most at heart in
the new Journal is to help in assisting the right
progress of these changes, by the cultivation of a
spirit of cheerfulness, reasonableness, and peace;
and the most special means which I look for to
this end, and which I earnestly desire on all sides,
from all parties and shades of party, or of no party
at all, is the countenance and co-operation of men
the most distinguished for genius and public spirit.
I hope they will deign to consider the Journal as
a kind of neutral ground, or academic grove and
resort of wit and philosophy, in which, while they
freely express thetr opinions, whatever those may
be, they will do so in accordance with the particular spirit of the place, and whether or not they
think it the best and most useful spirit to be
evinced at other times.

I could not give a better instance of what I
mean, than by referring to the encouragement

extended to my outset by my (in every sense of
the word) great friend Thomas Carlyle, who,
though I strongly differ with him respecting some
other great men, and though I had but lately
ventured some public remonstrances with his pre-
ference of that stormy to the sunny treatment of
existing human affairs, which he thinks necessary
to their well-being, has not only bid me God-speed
in my undertaking in a manner the most practical
and desirable, but answered those remonstrances
in such beautiful private words, as I only wish
delicacy could allow me to publish : they are so
full of that superiority to self-love, and that very
honey of kindness and goodness, which lie at the
core of all truly great hearts.

Such excellent things are sincerity and good
intention in the highest minds, or in any minds.
And so truly do they, and they only, enable a man
to discern them in others, and to pardon them
when differing with himself.

With respect to my own part in the Journal, it
is the first time in my life that, in a work of this
nature, I have had men of business at my side,
who, in addition to their power of assisting in the
literary portion, will give it those chances of circulation which can only be found in commercial
channels. The tone and temper of the articles which
I shall write, will be the same as in the Journal
which had nearly the same title ; and as to my
opinions, they will be expressed so entirely with
the usual freedom, that my readers will soon see
whether I continue to deserve the good wishes of
my friends the Many, or whether, and by which

of their conflicting judgments, I am to be esti-
mated according to certain of the Few; whether
as a person who would pull down all religion and
government; or whether as a person who would
set all up; or whether as a person who would set
them up this week, and pull them down the next;
or, on the other hand, just *vice versa* to that (purely
to oblige a gentleman who had a preconception to
that effect). All this I shall thankfully leave to
such trouble as the reader may choose to take on
the subject; myself having got tired of autobiographical statements of any kind, especially to
such differers with me in opinion as have made up
their minds publicly on the subject, and who therefore cannot afford to undo those very important
parcels. Some of these gentlemen come to the
most extraordinary conclusions, owing to mean
ideas which it would be a meanness to refute;
others for similar reasons "best known to themselves;" and some from sheer confusion of one
person with another. It has always been so, and
always will, as long as people are more uneasy at
giving up a mistake than doing justice.

My late admirable friend Thomas Campbell,
when I first knew him, was persuaded by one of
them to take me for Henry Hunt, the pike-parader
at Bristol. Not long since, Douglas Jerrold, of
whom I never uttered a word, public or private,
except in friendliness (due to him for his genius
and his long friendship for myself), was told by
another (who it was, I know not), that in something which I had said to the advantage of his wit
and popularity, I intended, not to praise, but to

abuse him ! And a little before this, a friend in a manufacturing town was informed that I was a terrible speculator in the money markets ! I, who was never in a market of any kind but to buy an apple or a flower, and who could not dabble in money dealings if I would, from sheer ignorance of their language.

But enough of enemies, for ever. Of friends, never. I confidently trust my undertaking in the hands of those, and of the public at large, feeling sure that they will not disapprove its spirit, whatever they may say to its power ; and hoping that the distinguished correspondents who commence with it, and other younger and to-be-distinguished ones whom I expect in their company, will save it from falling off, should my own strength be insufficient. I feel no abatement of it yet, thank God, as far as brain, or as heart and hope are concerned ; and success may give it me in respects less important.

The plan of the Journal will be seen from this first number ; and so

"Chi lo leggerà, viva felice."

May he, and she, that read it, live and prosper.

LEIGH HUNT.

House at Putney

Herbert Railton 1991.

CLASSIFIED BIBLIOGRAPHY.

CONTENTS.

CLASSIFIED BIBLIOGRAPHY.

I. NEWSPAPERS PROJECTED AND EDITED BY LEIGH HUNT.

I.

THE EXAMINER,[1] *A Sunday Paper on Politics, Domestic Economy, and Theatricals.* Motto : " Party is the madness of the many for the gain of the few."—SWIFT.

First number Jan. 3rd, 1808.

[There was a Monday issue, an almost exact reprint of the Sunday number. Published by John Hunt, edited by L. H. for the first thirteen years of its existence, and continued under other management up to Feb. 26th, 1881.

Here appeared, (besides numerous political and critical articles by Leigh Hunt),

(i.) 1809, a series of essays on *Methodism*, see No. 38.

(ii.) 1812, *March 22nd.* An article called *The Prince on St. Patrick's Day*, which brought about the imprisonment of John and Leigh Hunt from 1813-1815.

(iii.) *Jan.* 1815—*Jan.* 1817. Forty-eight essays

[1] The brothers Hunt had previously attempted to establish a paper, to be called "The Statesman."

called *The Round Table*, by L. H. and
Hazlitt, most of which were reprinted in
1817. See No. 53.

(iv.) 1821. *Sketches of Living Poets* —Bowles—
Byron—Campbell—Coleridge. L. H. had
intended to add Shelley and Keats.

(v.) *March 28th, 1824—Oct. 26th, 1825. The
Wishing Cap*, essays of which some were
reprinted in 1873 (No. 49), written at Maiano,
and inspired by a desire to return to London.
Containing some material for *The Town*.]

2. THE REFLECTOR, *A collection of Essays on
miscellaneous subjects of Literature and Politics, written by the Editor of the Examiner,
with the assistance of various other hands.*
Published as a quarterly magazine, 1810-
1812 ; collected in 2 vols., 1812.

[Here first appeared *The Feast of the Poets*, and
some of Lamb's best essays.]

3. THE INDICATOR. Motto : "A dram of sweet
is worth a pound of sour." Oct. 13th,
1819—March 21st, 1821 ; bound in 2 vols.,
1821.

[(The continuation of the series up to Oct. 13th,
1821, is not by L. H.) A weekly periodical, each
number containing an essay by L. H. and miscellaneous notes. Selections from these often . reprinted. He used the same title for his essays
(Nos. 77, 78, 80-84) in the *Literary Examiner*
(Nos. 79, 85-88 are not by him). No. 89 (by L. H.)
appeared in the *New Monthly Magazine*, 1832.

" Wit, poet, prose-man, party-man, translator,
Hunt, thy best title yet is *Indicator*."—*C. Lamb*.]

4. *The Literary Pocket-Book*, 1819-1822.

[An annual intended " to furnish a pocket memo-
randum book for intellectual observers and persons

of taste." Announced in the *Examiner*, 1818. "The verses marked Φ, are mine; Δ, Shelley's; P. R., Proctor's; and I, Keats's" (*letter from L. H. to C. Cowden Clarke*). Here appeared *The Calendar of the Seasons* reprinted as *the Months*, No. 39.]

5. THE LIBERAL. *Verse and Prose from the South.* 4 nos. 1822-1823. Bound in 2 vols., 1823.

[Contributions by Lord Byron, Shelley, and others. Written mainly in Italy, published in England by John Hunt. A description of Genoa, vol. i., p. 269, is reprinted without acknowledgment in *Life and Times of Lord Byron by an English Gentleman*," 1825.]

6. THE COMPANION. Jan. 9th—July 23rd, 1828. 28 nos. Motto : "The first quality in a Companion is Truth."—SIR W. TEMPLE.

[A weekly publication similar to the *Indicator*.]

7. CHAT OF THE WEEK, *a compendium of all Topics of Public Interest original and select.* Price 6*d.* Motto : "Veritas et Varietas." June 5th—Aug. 28th, 1830.

[In No. 8 the title was changed to *Chat of the Week and Gazette of Literature, Fine Arts, and Theatricals, price 7d.* But Government declared that, in its enlarged form, a stamp was necessary, and, as this could not be afforded, it was changed into—]

8. THE TATLER. *A Daily Journal of Literature and the Stage.* Motto : "Veritas et Varietas." Sept. 4th, 1830—Feb. 13th, 1832. Price 2*d.*

[Continued in other hands as a 'daily' till March 31st, when it was converted into a tri-weekly paper, and appeared up to Oct. 20th, 1832.

Each number contained four folio pages, and, except in case of his illness, was written entirely by

L. H. The work probably injured his health permanently.

THE PLAIN DEALER, announced in the *Tatler's* " Farewell to his readers," was never brought out.]

9. LEIGH HUNT'S LONDON JOURNAL. *To assist the enquiring, animate the struggling, and sympathize with all, comprising a great variety of original articles of an instructive and entertaining character by L. H., Esq., and many of his esteemed literary friends.* April 2nd, 1834—Dec. 31st, 1835.

[Brought out in partnership with Charles Knight. Joined with *The Printing Machine* June, 1835. 2 vols. folio. Contained :—supplements called 'The Streets of London' (incorporated in *The Town*, No. 57) — articles called 'The Week' — ' Birthdays of Eminent Men'— ' Romances of Real Life' (reprinted 1843, No. 73)—much material for ' *The Seer,*' ' *Men, Women, and Books,*' ' *Imagination and Fancy,*' ' *Wit and Humour.*'

About this Launcelot Cross wrote a delightfully enthusiastic little book, called *Characteristics of Leigh Hunt*, 1878.]

10. THE MONTHLY REPOSITORY. July, 1837—March, 1838.

[Originally a magazine in the Unitarian interest, but made unsectarian by L. H.'s editorial predecessors W. J. Fox and R. H. Horne. Here first appeared *The Blue-Stocking Revels.*]

11. LEIGH HUNT'S JOURNAL, *a miscellany for the cultivation of the memorable, the progressive, and the beautiful.* Dec. 7th, 1850—March 29th, 1851.

[First intended to be called *Leigh Hunt's London Magazine*. Here appeared *Lovers' Amazements*, and the *Streets of London* were continued.]

II. CONTRIBUTIONS TO OTHER PERIODICALS.

In :—

12. THE EUROPEAN MAGAZINE.

> [Poem called *Melancholy*, 1801.]

13. THE MONTHLY PRECEPTOR.

> [A magazine for young people. Through an essay in this, he became acquainted with the family of Marianne Kent, his future wife, about 1802.]

14. THE TRAVELLER, afterwards incorporated with the Globe.

> [Papers over signature Mr. Town junior, critic and censor-general. (Mr. Town, critic and censor-general, was the *nom de plume* of the authors of the *Connoisseur*, i.e. Bonnell Thornton and George Colman.) 1804-5.]

15. THE NEWS (a paper set up by John Hunt).

> [Theatrical Criticisms, 1805. Reprinted separately, 1807.]

16. THE TIMES.

> [Theatrical Criticisms, probably when L. H. was writing for his friend Barnes, who afterwards became managing editor: about 1807.]

17. THE NEW MONTHLY MAGAZINE. From its first appearance in 1821 till 1850.

> [Essays and poems over signatures H., Robin Goodfellow, Misocrotalus, many without any signature, and some with his name attached.
>
> In 1825, *The Family Journal*, signed H. H., *i.e.* Harry Honeycomb, who is supposed to be a de-

scendant of Will Honeycomb of *Spectator* memory.
Here occur the "imaginary conversations of Pope
and Swift," reprinted at the end of *Table Talk.*

In 1826 and 1827, *Some Specimens of a dictionary of Love and Beauty* (7 papers).

L. H. thought of reprinting some of the signed
poems that appeared in 1835 and 1836 under the
general title of *The Fabulous World*, but this
project was abandoned.

In *May*, 1832, *The Indicator*, No. 89.

In 1845, *Lazy Corner*, or *Bed versus Business.*

In 1850, several Poems reprinted in *Poetical
Works.*]

18. The Literary Examiner, *consisting of the
Indicator, a review of books, and some pieces
in prose and verse.*

[Announced in *Examiner*, June 29th, 1823, and
intended as a supplement for the fuller treatment
of literary subjects. Essays by L. H. under heading *Indicator*, between July and Sept. 1823—My
books, 2 papers—Suburbs of Genoa, 2 papers—
Latin Poems of Milton, 3 papers. The paper came
out July 5th—Dec. 27th, 1823.]

19. The Keepsake.

[Dreams on the borders of the land of poetry—
Pocket-books and Keepsakes, 1828. Identified by
Mr. J. Dykes Campbell, and reprinted in Mr.
Symons' volume of Selections.]

20. Bull's Court Magazine.

[*A Year of Honeymoons*, by Charles Dalton,
Esq. 8 papers, each dealing with one month.
1832-1833. Reprinted in Prof. Knight's *Tales
from Leigh Hunt.*]

21. True Sun Daily Review,

[Papers on various subjects, never reprinted.
Aug. 16th to Dec. 26th, 1833.]

22. TAIT'S MAGAZINE.

[A new series of *Wishing Cap Papers.* 6 papers. Jan.—Sept. 1833.]

23. THE WESTMINSTER REVIEW.

[Article on Lady Mary Wortley Montagu, being a review of Lord Wharncliffe's edition of her letters, &c. April, 1837.]

24. THE MUSICAL WORLD. *A Magazine of essays, critical and practical, and weekly record of musical science, literature, and intelligence.*

[Words for Composers—5 papers—Musician's Poetical Companion, 3 papers, being selections from the poets of songs suitable to be set to music, with comments. Jan. 10th to March 21st, 1839.]

25. THE MONTHLY CHRONICLE.

[Notes of a Lover of Books, 5 papers. Oct. 1838—Feb. 1839. L. H. originally intended one of these papers to begin with some reflections on suicide, and the omitted passage is printed in his " Correspondence," vol. ii., p. 327.

In 1840, Congratulatory Poems to the Queen.

The Magazine lasted through 7 vols. 1838— 1841.]

26. THE MONTHLY MAGAZINE.

[Poem—'A Rustic Walk and Dinner. Sept. 1842.]

27. THE EDINBURGH REVIEW.

[Reviews of Books :—Colman Family, Pepys Memoirs, Life and Letters of Madame Sévigné, George Selwyn and his contemporaries. 1841— 1844.]

28. AINSWORTH'S MAGAZINE.

['Jar of Honey from Mount Hybla.' Jan.

Dec. 1844, reprinted 1848—The Fancy Concert, 1845.]

29. ATLAS.

['Table Talk' over signature, Adam FitzAdam, Esq., 1846, reprinted in 1851. Streets of London, 1847, reprinted 1861, with title, *Saunter through the West End.*]

30. THE CAMBRIDGE CHRONICLE.

['Dirge for an Infant,' Feb. 3rd, 1849. It is unlikely that this is the first appearance of the poem, but I can find no earlier.—ED.]

31. THE MUSICAL TIMES *and singing class Circular.*

[Various prose papers. Dec. 1853—Nov. 1854.]

32. HOUSEHOLD WORDS.

[7 papers. 'Lounging through Kensington,' &c. Aug. 6th, 1853—Feb. 25th, 1854. Incorporated in first 12 chapters of *Old Court Suburb*, No. 58.]

33. THE NATIONAL MAGAZINE.

['Christmas Day, divided between two worlds: A fragment of a day-dream in the first heaven.' 1857.]

34. FRASER'S MAGAZINE.

[Feb., 'Tapiser's Tale'—May, 'Shewe of Fair Seeming'— Dec., 'English Poetry *v.* Cardinal Wiseman.' 1857.]

35. THE SPECTATOR.

[*The Occasional*, 16 papers. Jan. 15th to Aug. 20th, 1859. L. H. died Aug. 28th, 1859, and on Sept. 3rd, under the same heading, appeared a memorial paper by E[dmund] O[llier].]

36. TEMPLE BAR.
    ["*Men are but children of a larger growth.*"
    July, 1877.]

III. ESSAYS: COLLECTED.

[Nos. 37-44 were brought out by L. H. himself.]

37. CRITICAL ESSAYS ON THE PERFORMANCES
    OF THE LONDON THEATRES, *including
    general remarks on the practice and genius
    of the Stage, by the Editor of the Examiner.*
    1807.

    [Reprinted from the *News.* "To know an actor
    personally appeared to me a vice not to be thought
    of; and I would as lief have taken poison as ac-
    cepted a ticket from an actor."—*Autobiography.*
    Thus lightly did L. H. describe his introduction
    into theatrical criticism of an independent and im-
    .partial spirit.]

38. AN ATTEMPT TO SHOW THE FOLLY AND
    DANGER OF METHODISM. *In a series of
    essays, first published in the weekly paper
    called the Examiner, and now enlarged,
    with a preface and editorial notes, by the
    editor of the Examiner.* 1809.

39. THE MONTHS, *descriptive of the successive
    beauties of the year.* 1821.

    [First appeared as "*Calendar of the Seasons*"
    in the *Literary Pocket-Book.* Mrs. Southey made
    manuscript corrections of some botanical points,
    which are given in *Notes and Queries,* 4th series,
    vol. vi., p. 108.]

II.   R

40. INDICATOR AND COMPANION., Selected. 1834, often reprinted. The later editions being published with *The Seer.*

41. THE SEER. Motto : " Love adds a precious seeing to the eye." In 2 parts, 1840 and 1841. Reprinted as above, and in America,. 1864.

> [Collected from *London Journal—The Liberal — The Monthly Repository —The Tatler—The Round Table.* The Preface is "Given at this our suburban abode, with a fire on one side of us, and a vine at the window on the other, this 19th day of October, one thousand eight hundred and forty, in the very green and invincible year of our life the fifty-sixth.—L. H."]

42. MEN, WOMEN, AND BOOKS. *A selection of sketches, essays, and critical memoirs, from Leigh Hunt's uncollected prose writings,* 1847, 1852 ; and a cheap edition of 1870, often reprinted ; also in America.

> [The papers are taken from *The Westminster Review—The New Monthly Magazine—Tait's Magazine—Ainsworth's Magazine—The Monthly Chronicle.*]

43. A JAR OF HONEY FROM MOUNT HYBLA. 1848, 1870, 1882.

> [Illustrated by R. Doyle. Papers on Pastoral Poets, reprinted from *Ainsworth's Magazine.*]

44. TABLE TALK ; *to which are added imaginary conversations between Pope and Swift* (from Family Journal in *New Monthly Magazine*), 1851, 1858, etc. America, 1879.

> [The *Table Talk* appeared first in the *Atlas* and other periodicals.]

45. STUDIES EN SCHETSEN, *naar del Engelsch van Leigh Hunt door E. T. Polgieber.* Deventer, 1842.

    [A translation of some essays and tales by L. H.]

46. PROSE WORKS of Leigh Hunt. In 4 vols. America. [1857.]

47. A TALE FOR A CHIMNEY CORNER, *and other essays.* From 'the Indicator.' Edited by Edmund Ollier, with portrait, introduction, and notes. 1869; reprinted 1890 with title, "Essays by L. H.," without portrait.

48. A DAY BY THE FIRE, *and other papers.* Edited by J. E. B[abson]. 1870.

49. THE WISHING CAP PAPERS *from the Examiner, and other Essays.* Edited by J. E. B[abson].

    Boston, 1873; London, 1874.

50. ESSAYS; from the Indicator, Companion, Seer, and Keepsake. Edited by Arthur Symons, with introduction. 1888. (The Camelot Series.)

51. LEIGH HUNT AS POET AND ESSAYIST. Edited by Charles Kent, with introduction and portrait. 1889. (The Cavendish Library.)

    [An extensive collection, giving the original source of everything reprinted, but few of the essays are printed entire. A list of L. H.'s more important writings is given.]

52. TALES BY LEIGH HUNT. Edited by Prof.

Knight, with introduction and portrait. 1891.

Papers by Leigh Hunt will also be found in :—

53. (i) THE ROUND TABLE. *A collection of Essays on Literature, men, and manners.* By William Hazlitt. 2 vols., 1817, 1841. -

[Reprinted from *Examiner.* Papers by L. H., signed H. T. or L. H.]

54. (ii) ROMANCIST AND NOVELIST'S LIBRARY. Edited by William Hazlitt. 1839 and 1840.

55. (iii) HEADS OF THE PEOPLE. By Kenny Meadows. 1840, 1846.

[2 papers—'The Monthly Nurse' and 'The Omnibus Conductor.']

56. (iv) FALSTAFF'S LETTERS. *By James White, with notices of the author, collected from Charles Lamb, Leigh Hunt, and other contemporaries.*

[A reprint, 1877.
The part taken from L. H. appeared mostly in the *Indicator*, Jan. 24th, 1821.]

IV. LONDON GUIDE-BOOKS.

[In which the reader is taken "through London quarter by quarter, to notice the memorials as they arise;" and is delighted by gossip of unwearying brightness, largely derived from Pennant and *The Lounger's Common Place Book.*]

57. THE TOWN; *its memorable characters and events.* St. Paul's to St. James's. 2

vols. 1848 ; cheap edition of 1858 often reprinted.

[Much of this appeared first in *Leigh Hunt's London Journal*, and in *Leigh Hunt's Journal*. 45 illustrations.]

58. THE OLD COURT SUBURB. *Memorials of Kensington, regal, critical, and anecdotal.* 2 editions in 1855, 1860.

Largely reprinted from *Household Words*, 1853 and 1854.]

59. A SAUNTER THROUGH THE WEST END. 1861.

[Reprinted from the *Atlas*. 1847.]

V. VARIOUS PROSE WORKS.

60. REFORMIST'S REPLY TO AN ARTICLE IN THE EDINBURGH REVIEW. 1810.

["A Pamphlet in defence of its own reforming principles."—*Autobiography.*]

61. A FULL REPORT OF THE TRIAL OF JOHN AND LEIGH HUNT, *Proprietors of the Examiner, on an information filed ex-officio by the Attorney-General, decided by Lord Ellenborough and a special Jury in the King's Bench, Westminster, on Wednesday, the 9th of December,* 1812 ; *to which are added observations on the Trial, by the Editor of the Examiner.* [1813.]

[The "observations" are taken from the *Examiners* of December, 1812, January and February, 1813, and I therefore date the pamphlet 1813 instead of 1812, as has been previously done.]

62. MUSICAL COPYRIGHT. *Proceedings on a trial before the Hon. Baron George, in the Court of Exchequer, Dublin, May 18th, 1815, in the cause, Whitaker versus Hime ; to which are subjoined observations on the extraordinary defence made by Mr. Sergeant Joy, counsel for the Defendant, by Leigh Hunt, Esq.* 1816.

[It seems that Mr. Sergeant Joy took occasion to attack the *immorality* of Leigh Hunt's songs, which Whitaker had set to music (see this Bibliography, No. 110). L. H. of course denies the charge, and draws attention to its irrelevancy. His remarks are reprinted from the 'Examiner.']

63. CHRISTIANISM, *or Belief and unbelief reconciled, being exercises and meditations.* 1832.

[A manual of domestic devotion, printed only for private circulation. 75 copies.
Written in Italy (1824) at a time of great depression, and at the request and expense of John Forster, who wrote an anonymous preface to it.]

64. RELIGION OF THE HEART. *A Manual of Faith and Duty.* 1853.

[An enlarged reprint of No. 63, being an unsectarian kind of prayer-book. Mr. C. W. Reynell possesses a copy of this, which L. H. had corrected for a 2nd edition.]

65. SIR RALPH ESHER, *or the Memoirs of a Gentleman of the Court of Charles the Second, including those of his Friend, Sir Philip Herne.* 1832, 1836, 1850.

66. LORD BYRON AND SOME OF HIS CONTEMPO-

RARIES, *with recollections of the author's life and his visit to Italy.* 1 vol. 4to, 2 vols. 8vo, with index, Paris, and Philadelphia. 1828.

[Besides the matter about Byron, and the strictly autobiographical chapters, this book contains reminiscences of Lamb, Shelley, Keats, Moore, Coleridge, the brothers Smith, &c., and portraits of Lord Byron, Countess Guiccioli, Keats, Lamb, and Leigh Hunt.

Most of the matter is reprinted in the *Autobiography.*]

Extracts from the above may be found in :—

(i) OPERE COMPLETE DI LORD BYRON *voltate dall' originale inglese in prosa italiana da Carlo Ruseoni con note et illustrazioni del volgarizzatore* . . . . *nonchè dei signori Moore, Walter Scott* . . . . *Hunt, etc.* Padova, 1842.

(ii) THE TRUE STORY OF LORD AND LADY BYRON *as told by* [*various persons*] *in answer to Mrs. Beecher Stowe.* 1869.

[A very quaint collection of pamphlets.]

67. AUTOBIOGRAPHY AND REMINISCENCES *of friends and contemporaries.* In 3 vols., with a portrait in each; 1850 and 1852. In 1 vol., with a new portrait ; 1860.

[The 1860 edition is revised by the author, with further revision, and an introduction by his eldest son (Thornton Hunt). A cheap edition without the portrait was published in the same year, and has been often reprinted in England and America.]

68. CORRESPONDENCE of Leigh Hunt.　2 vols.,
1862.　Edited by Thornton Hunt.

[Including part of a Journal (addressed to "My
dear children ") of his days in gaol.

A third volume was projected, to be edited by
Lord Brougham. When the manuscripts came
into the hands of Mr. Townsend Mayer, he published with comments some additional letters under
the following titles:—"Leigh Hunt and B. R.
Haydon," "Leigh Hunt and Dr. Southwood
Smith," "Leigh Hunt and Charles Ollier," in the
St. James' Magazine, vol. xxxiv., p. 349, vol. xxxv.,
p. 76, vol. xxxv., p. 387 respectively, and "Leigh
Hunt and Lord Brougham" in Temple Bar, June
1876.

Many of L. H.'s letters may be also found in
"Recollections of Writers," by Charles and Mary
Cowden Clarke, and a long and interesting one
to Robert Browning in the Athenæum, July 7th,
1883.]

VI. SELECTIONS FROM OTHER WRITERS AND CRITICAL BIOGRAPHIES.

69. CLASSIC TALES, *serious and lively, a selection
from English and foreign authors, with
critical essays on the merits and reputations
of the authors.*

First published in 15 parts.　Bound in
5 vols. ; the first dated 1806, and the others
1807.[1]　Reprinted 1813.

[L. H. wrote the preface, selected and wrote all

---

[1] Or sometimes, apparently, all dated 1807.

the introductory essays (to which his initials are signed) except those on Marmontel, Hawkesworth, and Sterne, which Mr. Ireland believes to have been written by Mr. C. H. Reynell. The following have been lately reprinted in separate volumes by Messrs. Paterson and Sons—Voltaire, Goldsmith and Brooke, Marmontel, John Mackenzie and Sterne, Hawkesworth.]

70. MASQUE OF ANARCHY by Shelley. 1832.

[Preface by L. H.]

71. THE DRAMATIC WORKS OF WYCHERLEY, CONGREVE, VANBURGH, AND FARQUHAR, *with Biographical and critical notices by Leigh Hunt.* 1840, 1851.

[The prefatory matter includes Lamb's essay on "The Artificial Comedy of the last century," and Hazlitt's essay on the four dramatists.]

72. SHERIDAN'S WORKS. Moxon, 1840, 1848.

[With Biographical and critical sketch by L. H.]

73. ONE HUNDRED ROMANCES OF REAL LIFE *selected and annotated by Leigh Hunt, comprising remarkable historical and domestic facts, illustrative of human nature.* 1843, 1888.

[Reprinted from *London Journal*, and largely taken from *The Lounger's Common Place Book*.]

74. IMAGINATION AND FANCY, *or selections from the English poets illustrative of those first requisites of their art, with markings of the best passages, critical notices of the writers and an essay in answer to the question,*

'*What is Poetry?*' 1844, 1845, 1852; a cheap edition of 1870 often reprinted.

[L. H. first intended to call this volume *True Poetry*, and the manuscript draft of it is now in the possession of Mr. Ireland.]

75. WIT AND HUMOUR. *Selected from the English poets, with an illustrative essay and critical comments.* 1846, 1852; a cheap edition of 1870 often reprinted.

[In preface to No. 74 we read, "the Editor proposes to give in succession corresponding volumes of the Poetry of Action and Passion (narrative and dramatic) from Chaucer to Campbell—of Contemplation, from Surrey to Campbell—of Wit and Humour, from Chaucer to Byron—of Song or lyrical poetry, from Chaucer again to Campbell and Burns and O'Keefe." Of these, however, only the two (Nos. 74 and 75) were published.]

76. THE FOSTER BROTHERS. A novel by Thornton Hunt. [1845.]

[With a very brief preface by L. H.]

77. STORIES FROM THE ITALIAN POETS. 1846, 1854. New York, 1848.

[The stories of the most important poems of Dante, Pulci, Boiardo, Ariosto, and Tasso, told in prose, with biographical and critical introductions.

Two volumes of selections from this came out in the "Knickerbocker Nuggets," 1888, and part of the Introduction to Dante is reprinted in the notes of Longfellow's translation of the "Divina Commedia.']

78. A BOOK FOR A CORNER, *or selections in prose and verse from authors the best suited to that mode of enjoyment, with comments on each, and a general introduction.* 80 wood engravings. 2 vols. 1849; 1 vol. 1851, 1858.

79. READINGS FOR RAILWAYS, *or anecdotes and other short stories, reflections, maxims, characteristics, passages of wit, humour, and poetry, etc. Together with points of information on matters of general interest collected in the course of his own reading.* (Preface dated Dec. 1st, 1849.)   1850.

80. READINGS FOR RAILWAYS.   1853.

[Another series with the same full title as the above, by L. H. and J. B. Syme.]

81. BEAUMONT AND FLETCHER, *or the finest scenes, lyrics, and other beauties of those two poets, now first selected from the whole of their works, to the exclusion of whatever is morally objectionable; with opinions of distinguished critics, notes, explanatory and otherwise, and a general introductory preface.*   1855.

82. BOOK OF THE SONNET.   Edited by Leigh Hunt and S. Adams Lee.   2 vols.   1867. London and Boston.

[Vol. I. English Sonnets.   A prefatory essay on poetry by L. H., his introductory letter to S. Adams Lee, and a few of his sonnets.

Vol. II. American Sonnets.   Essay by S. Adams Lee.]

83. SHELLEY'S WORKS.   Early Poems.   1871.

[With memoir of Shelley by L. H.   Reprinted from ' Lord Byron and his Contemporaries.']

[*Note.*—When in Italy, Leigh Hunt wished to bring out a selection of modern English literature, but the Italian bookseller refused to publish the book, being in fear of the authorities.]

VII. POETRY: SEPARATE POEMS.

84. STORY OF RIMINI. 1816, 1817, 1819.

> [Reprinted in altered form in *Poetical Works.*]

85. HERO AND LEANDER AND BACCHUS AND ARIADNE. 1819.

> [The volume contained also 'The Panther.' 'Hero and Leander' has been often reprinted in an abbreviated form; and *one* passage from Bacchus and Ariadne may be found in *Poetical Works*, 1832, and in *Rimini and other poems.*]

86. ULTRA CREPIDARIUS. *A satire on Gifford, to which are appended extracts from Hazlitt's letter to Gifford.* 1823.

87. BACCHUS IN TUSCANY. *A Dithyrambic Poem, from the Italian of Francesco Redi, with notes original and select.* 1825.

> [Reprinted in *Poetical Works.* Some specimens of this with an account of the author appeared in *The Companion*, June 18th, 1828.]

88. CAPTAIN SWORD AND CAPTAIN PEN. *With some remarks on War and Military Statesmen.* 8 illustrations. 1835, 1839, 1849.

> [Revised and reprinted in *Poetical Works.*]

89. BLUE STOCKING REVELS. n.d.

> [On the authority of Lowndes' and Allibones' Bibliographical Dictionaries.]

90. THE PALFREY. *A love story of old times.* 1842.

> [6 illustrations. Stolen by American and Parisian papers on its first appearance. Reprinted in *Poetical Works.*]

91. Poems of L. H. will also be found in :—

> (*a*) POEMS OF CHAUCER MODERNIZED.
> 1841.
>
> [Contains 3 by L. H.—The Manciple's Tale—
> The Friar's Tale—The Squire's Tale.]
>
> (*b*) THE POETICAL REGISTER *or Repository of Fugitive Poetry*, for 1801, 1805,
> 1806-1807, 1808-1809, 1810-1811.

VIII. POETRY : COLLECTED.

92. JUVENILIA, *or a collection of Poems; written between the ages of twelve and sixteen by J. H. L. Hunt, late of the Grammar School of Christ's Hospital, and dedicated by permission to the Hon. J. H. Leigh, containing Miscellanies, Translations, Sonnets, Pastorals, Elegies, Odes, Hymns, and Anthems.* 2 editions in 1801 ; 3rd ed. 1802 ; 1803 [also called the 3rd] ; 1804 [called the 4th].

93. THE FEAST OF THE POETS. *With notes, and other pieces in verse by the editor of the Examiner.* 1814, 1815.

> [Some copies of the first edition were struck off
> with date 1815. L. H.'s name appears on title-
> page of 2nd edition, which was "amended and en-
> larged." *The Feast of the Poets* is reprinted in an
> enlarged and modified form from the *Reflector*, 1812.]

94. FOLIAGE, *or poems original and translated.*
1818.

> [Some copies of this were struck off with date
> 1819. The volume is divided into *Greenwoods*, or
> original poems, and *Evergreens*, or translations
> from Poets of Antiquity.]

95. RIMINI, *and other poems.* Boston, 1844.

96. STORIES IN VERSE. *Now first collected.* 1855.

97. FAVOURITE POEMS. Boston, 1877 and in *Modern Classics*, 1881-2.

98. POEMS OF LEIGH HUNT AND THOMAS HOOD. 1889.

> [Edited by J. Harwood Panting, *Canterbury Poets.*]

'POETICAL WORKS':—

99. A. In 3 vols. 1819.

> [Being Nos. 84 and 104, 85 and 93, and 94, bound together with separate title-pages.]

100. B. In 1 vol. 1832.

> [Being the first collected edition, published by subscription.]

101. C. In 1 vol. *Containing many pieces now first collected.* 1844, 1846, and 1888.

> [Including the 'Legend of Florence.']

102. D. In 2 vols. *Revised by himself, and edited with an introduction by S. Adams Lee.* Boston, 1857, 1866.

> [With the 'Legend of Florence' and 'Lovers' Amazements.']

103. E. In 1 vol. *Now finally collected, revised by himself, and edited by his son, Thornton Hunt, with illustrations by Corbould.* 1860.

> [Not in any way a complete edition, with no plays. Also printed in America.]

IX. DRAMATIC PIECES.

[" The propensity to dramatic writing had been strong in me from boyhood."]

104. DESCENT OF LIBERTY, *a mask, to which is prefixed an account of the origin and nature of masks.* 1815, 1816.

105. AMYNTAS, *a tale of the woods, from the Italian of Torquato Tasso.* 1820.

['Ode to the Golden Age,' from this, has been often reprinted.]

106. LEGEND OF FLORENCE, a play in 5 acts. 1840.

[Reprinted in *Poetical Works*, 1844 and 1857, in G. H. Lewes' *Selections from Modern British Dramatists*, 1861, and in America. Performed several times at Covent Garden, at Windsor Castle in 1852, and at Manchester in 1859.

" *The Legend of Florence, as first written, did not conclude with the death of the husband. He was dismissed into a monastery; and the wife was married to her first lover by a 'special license' of the Pope, as in the original story; a very special license from that quarter, but suggesting, I think, a more touching as well as a more refined and dramatic treatment.*"—LETTER TO S. ADAMS LEE IN POETICAL WORKS, 1857.]

107. LOVERS' AMAZEMENTS, *or How will it end?* 1850.

[Printed in *Leigh Hunt's Journal* and *Poetical Works*, 1857.]

108. THREE UNPUBLISHED PLAYS.

Secret Marriage, since called the *Prince's Marriage*.

The Double, prose and verse, 2 acts.
Look to your morals, prose after-piece.
[See *Autobiography,* p. 391.]

X. FRAGMENTS.

109.   [In addition to the above WORKS of Leigh Hunt
the following single pieces may be found in the
Correspondence:—Poetical Epistle to Miss Ma-
rianne Kent, Feb. 1806—Rhymes to his daughter
Jacintha, 1843—Poem on his son Vincent's death,
1852—Inscription for bust of Dr. Southwood Smith,
1856—To a lady who wished to see him, from the
French of Marot, 1859.]

110. THREE SONGS by Leigh Hunt were published
separately, being set to music by *Whitaker.*

[*Love and the Æolian Harp,* 1808 (printed also
in the *Correspondence*).
Silent Kisses. [1809.]
Mary, Mary, List awake. 1809.
There are 2 copies of the last in the British
Museum, printed without the music, in which the
words are not exactly the same.]

XI. MANUSCRIPTS.[1]

111. TRUE POETRY, the first draft of 'Imagination and Fancy.'

· [In the possession of Mr. Ireland, who has also
made copies of the following :—]

112. FRAGMENTS.
A Prose piece, (about quiet pleasure,)

[[1] The manuscripts marked with an asterisk are printed
in these volumes.—ED.]

Aug. 19th, 1837; Faith, Hope, and Charity, and the Prospects of Manhood, a poem ;* To Viscount Stopford, a congratulatory poem ; Alive,* prose ; The Religion of a Lover of Truth ;* Pleasant Thoughts for Pleasant People, No. 1 ; From Dante, two verses ;* an "unrhymed yet undramatic" and irregular verse ;* The Melancholy Lover to his Mistress, poem ;* Argument in brief quatrain ; Town Amusements, No. 1 ; Twelfth Night, A dramatic sketch.

113. In the Dyce and Forster Library, South Kensington.

   A Review of Dr. Fellowe's Religion of the Universe ; and *Calviultor,** sonnet written in the character of a bald man in answer to a clever sonnet against baldness.

114. In the same place is a printed list of the *locks of hair* in the possession of L. H., as marked in his own handwriting, concerning some of which he wrote in the "*New Wishing Cap.*"

115. *Annotations of many books in his library.* Mostly in the possession of Mrs. Fields, of Boston.

116. *Letters of Pliny the Younger,* 1751, with manuscript notes by L. H. In the British Museum.

INDEX TO BIBLIOGRAPHY,

CHRONOLOGICALLY ARRANGED.[1]

[1 An asterisk is prefixed to those books of which an edition is in print.]

1834.	Indicator and Companion (Selections). [No. 40.]
1834-5.	Leigh Hunt's London Journal. [No. 9.]
1835.	Captain Sword and Captain Pen. [No. 88.]
1837.	Articles in Westminster Review. [No. 23.]
1837-8.	Monthly Repository. [No. 10.]
n. d.	Blue Stocking Revels. [No. 89.]
1838-9.	Articles in Monthly Chronicle. [No. 25.]
1839.	Articles in Musical World. [No. 24.]
1839.	Tales in Romancist and Novelist's Library. [No. 54.]
1840.	Heads of the People. [No. 55.]
1840.	Legend of Florence. [No. 106.]
1840.	Wycherley, Congreve, Vanburgh, and Farquhar edited. [No. 71.]
1840.	Sheridan, preface to. [No. 72.]
1840-1.	Seer. [No. 41.]
1841.	Chaucer modernized. [No. 91.]
1841.	Articles in Monthly Chronicle. [No. 25.]
1841-4.	Articles in Edinburgh Review. [No. 27.]
1842.	Palfrey. [No. 90.]
1842.	Studies en Schetsen. [No. 45.]
1842.	Poem in Monthly Magazine. [No. 26.]
*1843.	Hundred Romances of Real Life. [No. 73.]
1844.	Jar of Honey, in Ainsworth's Magazine. [No. 28.]
*1844.	Poetical Works. [No. 101.]

1857.   Articles in Fraser's Magazine. [No. 34.]

1859.   The Occasional in Spectator. [No. 35.]

1860.   Poetical Works. [No. 103.]

*1860.   Autobiography (new edition). [No. 67.]

1861.   Saunter through West End. [No. 59.]_

1862.   Correspondence. [No. 68.]

1867.   Book of the Sonnet. [No. 82.]

*1869.   Tale for a Chimney Corner. [No. 47.]

1870.   A Day by the Fire. [No. 48.]

*1871.   Memoir of Shelley. [No. 83.]

1873.   Wishing Cap Papers. [No. 49.]

1877.   Favourite Poems. [No. 97.]

1877.   Paper in Temple Bar. [No. 36.]

1877.   Falstaff's Letters. [No. 56.]

*1888.   Essays (Camelot Series). [No. 50.]

*1889.   Poems of L. H. and Thomas Hood. [No. 98.]

*1889.   Leigh Hunt as Poet and Essayist. [No. 51.]

*1891.   Tales by Leigh Hunt. [No. 52.]

BOOKS THAT HAVE BEEN WRONGLY ATTRIBUTED TO LEIGH HUNT.

Tales from Boccaccio, with modern illustrations, and other poems.   1846.

[Written by some person who was apparently contemplating suicide, and who had been with Lord Byron at Ravenna. A copy of the book was presented by the author to T. Chapman, F.R.S.]

Florentine Tales.   1847.
Which contains the above.

A Philosophical Dictionary, from the French of M. de Voltaire.   In 6 vols.   1824.
Published by J. and H. L. Hunt.

[Written, as Mr. Ireland kindly pointed out to me, by John Gorton, author of "A General Biographical Dictionary," 1828. See *The Dictionary of National Biography.*]

An Historical and Critical Dictionary.   Selected and abridged from the great work of Peter Bayle, with a life of the author.   In 4 vols.   1826.

Translations from French Poets. To which are appended extracts from the Tourist's Journal, etc., by the author of "Critical Essays," etc. 1845.

[The same author also brought out a translation of " Béranger" in 1839.   Preface dated from Brighton.]

Eliza Cook's Journal, Nov. 1850, credits L. H. with editing the *Monthly Reporter*, and Charles Knight's *Encyclopædia* says that he wrote for the *London Magazine.* It has been also stated that he edited Fairfax's translation of "Jerusalem Delivered." The report probably arose from the two facts that the Rev. J. H. Hunt (fellow of Trinity College, Cambridge) published a translation of Tasso in 1818, and that Leigh Hunt wrote a paper called "Hoole's and Fairfax's Tasso," in the *Indicator*, March 29th, 1820.

LIST OF PORTRAITS.[1]

["He was rather tall, as straight as an arrow, and looked slenderer than he really was. His hair was black and shining, and slightly inclined to wave; his head was high, his forehead straight and white, his eyes black and sparkling, his general complexion dark. There was in his whole carriage and manner an extraordinary degree of life."—THORNTON HUNT, *Introduction to Autobiography*, 1860.

"Dark complexion (a trace of the African, I believe), copious clean strong black hair, beautifully-shaped head, fine beaming serious hazel eyes; seriousness and intellect the main expression of the face (to our surprise at first); he would lean on his elbow against the mantelpiece (fine, clean, elastic figure too he had, five feet ten or more), and look round him nearly in silence, before taking leave for the night, 'as if I were a Lar,' said he once, 'or permanent household god here!' (such his polite aerial way)."—THOMAS CARLYLE, *Reminiscences*.]

1. BOWYER, miniature painter to the King. ½ length. Full face. Aged 17 (1801). An engraving by Parker in *Juvenilia*, 1802, and subsequent editions, by G. H. Ford in *Autobiography*, vol. i., 1850. [Rather conventional.—ED.]

---

[1] Except when otherwise indicated, the opinions expressed about these portraits have been derived from Mr. Walter Leigh Hunt. They have been arranged chronologically, as far as the dates are known.

2. JACKSON. ½ length, ¾ face. Engraving by Freeman to be seen at the print-room of the British Museum and in print shops. ["In the manner of that artist, imparting to it a lazy heaviness, said to have characterized the artist, but certainly foreign to the sitter."—Thornton Hunt, *Autobiography.*]

3. WAGEMAN. Pencil sketch. ¾ length, ¾ face. Photographed by Guilo Rossi, Milan, and reproduced in *The Century*, March, 1882, and in *Scribner's Magazine*, March, 1888. [Drawn at the request of Vincent Novello when L. H. left prison in 1815.]

4. MARGARET GILLIES. ⅛ length, ¾ face. Reproduced in the *People's Journal*, 1846, and the *Eclectic Magazine*, Nov., 1846. [Very poor—taken in youth.]

5. SEVERN. Unfinished miniature. Head. ¾ face. Engraving by G. H. Ford in *Autobiography*, vol. ii., 1850, and by J. C. Armytage, in *Men, Women, and Books*, 1847, and to be seen in print-shops. ["Only a sketch on a small scale, but it suggested the kindness and animation of his countenance." Thornton Hunt, *Introduction to Autobiography.*]

6. WILDMAN. Chalk-drawing. ⅛ length. [This perished, unfortunately, as it was "one of the best taken in early life."—Thornton Hunt, *Introduction to Autobiography.*]

7. B. R. HAYDON. Bust portrait; life-size, ½ length, ¾ face. In National Portrait Gallery. [About 1821. Missing all the mobile fascination and gentle fire of the face.]

8. J. HAYTER. ½ length, ¾ face. Engraving

by H. Meyer in *Lord Byron and His Contemporaries*, 1828, and in *Indicator and Companion*, 1835 (to be seen at the print-room of the British Museum and in print-shops), by H. Wright Smith in *American Edition of L. H.'s Poems*, 1857, by an unnamed engraver in *Favourite Poems*, 1877. Etching by M. Lalange in *Tales from Leigh Hunt*, 1891. ["I have only one more opinion to guard against . . . . to wit, the face which the engraver in his hurry has been pleased to thrust upon me, and which might lead people to suppose that I am not only capable of calumniating my host, but of walking off with his tankard. . . . . My face is rescued from insignificance solely by thought ; but I must really be allowed to say, that there is nothing in it which ought to take me to Bow Street."—Appendix to 2nd edit. of *Lord Byron and his Contemporaries*.]

9. DANIEL MACLISE, R.A. Full-length engraving, leaning against a wall, swallow-tail coat, hat and gloves in left hand. In *Fraser's Magazine*, June, 1834, being one of a " *Gallery of Illustrious Literary Men*," which the artist published with signature "A. Croquis," and which was republished in book form 1873. [Tinged by caricature, and not characteristic.]

10. SAMUEL LAWRENCE, unfinished, ¾ length, sitting. Full face. In possession of the artist's executors. Exhibited at the Guelph Exhibition. 1837. Reproduced by photography in *Correspondence*, 1862, in *The Art Journal*, October, 1865, and in *Scribner's Magazine*, March, 1888. [The most satisfactory of the portraits in every way.]

11. A sketch for the above, in the possession of Mr. Walter Leigh Hunt, is reproduced in the present work.

12. MRS. GLIDDON. Bust portrait. Profile. Aged 57 (1841). "Now drawn on wood by Mr. C. Gliddon" for *A Tale for a Chimney Corner*, 1869. [A fair likeness, but very unattractive.]

13. W. F. WILLIAMS. Head and shoulders. ¾ face. Aged 66 (1850). Engraving by J. C. Armytage in *Autobiography*, 1860, *Leigh Hunt as Poet and Essayist*, 1890, and Baines' *History of Hampstead*. [Agreeable, but too weak.]

14. G. H. FORD. On stone, from life. ½ length. Full face. Aged 66 (1850). In *Autobiography*, vol. iii., 1850. [Pleasing, but not sufficiently animated, particularly as regards the eyes.]

CHISWICK PRESS :—C. WHITTINGHAM AND CO., TOOKS COURT, CHANCERY LANE.